Get Set for Study Abroad

Titles in the GET SET FOR UNIVERSITY series:

Get Set for American Studies
ISBN 0 7486 1692 6

Get Set for Communication Studies
ISBN 0 7486 2029 X

Get Set for Computer Science
ISBN 0 7486 2167 9

Get Set for English Language
ISBN 0 7486 1544 X

Get Set for English Literature
ISBN 0 7486 1537 7

Get Set for History
ISBN 0 7486 2031 1

Get Set for Media and Cultural Studies
ISBN 0 7486 1695 0

Get Set for Nursing
ISBN 0 7486 1956 9

Get Set for Philosophy
ISBN 0 7486 1657 8

Get Set for Politics
ISBN 0 7486 1545 8

Get Set for Psychology
ISBN 0 7486 2096 6

Get Set for Religious Studies
ISBN 0 7486 2032 X

Get Set for Sociology
ISBN 0 7486 2019 2

Get Set for Study Abroad
ISBN 0 7486 2030 3

Get Set for Study in the UK
ISBN 0 7486 1810 4

Get Set for Teacher Training
ISBN 0 7486 2139 3

Get Set for Study Abroad

Tom Barron

Edinburgh University Press

Edinburgh University Press Ltd
22 George Square, Edinburgh

Typeset in Sabon
by Servis Filmsetting Ltd, Manchester, and
printed and bound in Great Britain by William Clowes Ltd, Beccles, Suffolk

A CIP Record for this book is available from the British Library

ISBN 0 7486 2030 3 (paperback)

CONTENTS

ACKNOWLEDGEMENTS

Each chapter of the book begins with a couple of quotations from students reporting on their experience of Study Abroad. These are real opinions, culled from questionnaires issued to students in the University of Edinburgh at the end of their time abroad. A few verbal changes have been made in some of them, partly for stylistic reasons, partly to remove any possibility of the author being identifiable. All these questionnaires were completed anonymously but an extra safeguard still seemed sensible. None the less, I have tried to ensure that what is quoted captures precisely the sense of the original. I want to thank the students whose quotations I have used and all the others who are not quoted but whose views have enhanced my understanding and influenced much of what is written here. I also want to thank the University of Edinburgh for its co-operation and assistance (not to mention gainful employment over many years) which enabled the work to be researched and then completed.

My greatest debt is to my former colleagues in the International Office at Edinburgh whose help, advice and cheerfulness saw me through this project. In particular, I must thank Sandra Morris, Acting Director and European Co-ordinator, whose knowledge of Study Abroad is encyclopaedic and who taught me most of what I know about the subject. Lesley Balharry, the European desk officer, who read a section in typescript, and Alan Mackay, with his expertise in North America, were also very helpful; and Helen, Clare, Kirsty, Ann, Kerry, Stacey, Jane, Mark and Adilia all chipped in generously. Craig Mathieson, my successor as Director, gave me his assistance and encouragement at a difficult time for him.

I must also record my thanks to the two anonymous readers of the typescript for Edinburgh University Press, who made several helpful suggestions which I have adopted, and to colleagues elsewhere, particularly Peter Whitelaw of Queen Margaret University College who read and commented on parts of the work. Nicola Ramsey of EUP provided ideas and guidance. The section on intercultural relations and study skills owes a good deal to a UKCOSA workshop, organised by Alison Barty, which made much profitable use of Colin Lago and Alison Barty's *Working with International Students* (2nd edition, 2003, published by UKCOSA). Thanks go to Alison, the workshop leaders and its participants. As always, I have pestered the students from Pomona College in California, for whom I act as local Programme Director during their semester in Edinburgh, to provide me with their advice. I am grateful to them, particularly Ellen Perkins, and to Susan Popko of Pomona's Study Abroad Office. I am also indebted to Jim Strachan who showed huge interest and much concern for the work. But only I, of course, am responsible for any errors or inaccuracies which, in defiance of such skilled assistance, still remain.

1 INTRODUCTION

If you are a student in the United Kingdom, you have the opportunity to study abroad. It can be a really worthwhile experience, enjoyable, exhilarating and enlightening. It can also be difficult and frustrating. Getting to grips with studying in another country is not simple though the rewards are great if you succeed. Those who have experienced it often feel they have gained a good deal. They claim to have acquired a more balanced appreciation of different cultures, and a skill and sensitivity in dealing with cultural issues which has enhanced their subsequent studies. Some even suggest that the opportunity to study abroad has opened their eyes to the outside world and made them feel more like true global citizens. But because Study Abroad is not without its challenges, everyone is agreed that, to get the most out of it, you have to prepare carefully, to know what you are taking on and to be ready to take advantage of the opportunities that arise. That is what this book is about.

If you do decide that you would like to study abroad, it is no longer difficult to arrange. It is not necessary to do all the work of setting things up yourself. There are dozens of programmes available which have the approval of the universities and colleges in the United Kingdom. You don't need to be concerned about identifying places abroad which would be good for your studies. That is done for you. You don't have to worry about different curricula or different marking systems. Your own university will have decided what you need to do and how your work will be assessed. All you have to do is to discover what is available and what will suit you best. And you then have to make up your mind to apply. This book is designed to help you with this decision and to give you a sense of what might be involved once the decision is made.

Study Abroad is the term generally used nowadays for programmes that allow students in one country to do part of their degree studies in another. Despite its widespread use, it can cause confusion. It is obviously meant to indicate that the main purpose of the programmes is to enable you to study outside your own country. But many students who go abroad to study are seeking an overseas degree, which Study Abroad students usually are not. Other terms have also been employed – visiting study, occasional study, non-graduating study – to make this distinction clear. But they, too, have their weaknesses. As a Study Abroad student, you are not simply visiting another university, you are studying there. Nor are you studying only on occasions (or at least it is hoped not) but on a full-time basis. And you certainly will have the intention of graduating, even if not at your host institution. 'Study Abroad' has probably become accepted only as the least misleading term.

The key element in these programmes which the term misses is that your studies abroad can count towards your degree at home. Whatever courses you take or projects you complete can replace whatever you would have been required to do had you remained at home. You don't normally have to take work abroad with you and you don't normally have to catch up on what you have missed when you return. The overseas work substitutes entirely for the work at home and is held to be equivalent to it in almost every way.

Over the last two decades, Study Abroad has become much more popular and its academic value more widely appreciated. Where once it was largely undertaken only by language students, it is now often a requirement for other degree subjects, particularly those with an immediate vocational relevance, like engineering or business, and those with a strongly international curriculum, like fine art or area studies. But the largest growth has been the result of students opting for Study Abroad not because it is a requirement but simply for its own sake.

This book is intended to help everyone contemplating studying abroad or confronted by the need to do so and who perhaps knows little of what is involved. It is designed for students at college or university who are considering Study Abroad as an option and for those still at school who want to know something about this opportunity within higher and further education. It is aimed particularly at those who are thinking of taking on international study for the first time. But the idea is to conduct you through the whole process, so that the book can also serve after you embark on the study. The focus is largely on undergraduates, though some sections will also have an interest for postgraduates. It is hoped that schools counsellors, parents and officials involved in advising students going abroad may also find here something of use.

2 STUDY ABROAD

'I find that a new university and a new approach to my subject have given me a new enthusiasm and interest in my studies, and I've had opportunities I never would have had at home.'

'There are some awful moments but the most important thing is not to panic.'

Study Abroad is currently undertaken by only a minority of UK students. Though much has been done to encourage others to take it on, there is clearly a general concern about breaking with tradition and launching out into something less familiar. At the same time, school travel, gap years and globalisation are making the rest of the world much more open and accessible to everyone. The opportunities are clearly there. To be able to realise them, you first need to take stock of what is to be gained. This chapter looks at the principal reasons which students give for studying abroad and why universities and governments are enthusiastic in offering their support.

WHY STUDY ABROAD?

There are many reasons for studying abroad. For nearly everyone, the primary appeal is academic, to deepen your knowledge and enhance your understanding. Undertaking some of your studies in another country offers you a new insight into, and a wider appreciation of, your subject or discipline. That is evidently the case when a period of Study Abroad is a requirement of your degree. But it applies much more generally, too. Many subjects have almost naturally an international dimension.

All the humanities, social sciences and applied sciences do, for example, because they all deal with culture and society. Studying in a different country brings an extra perspective to them. For other areas of study, the main purpose is usually to discover what your subject gains when the context and presentation are new. Most students think these gains considerable. It helps that academic life world-wide is sufficiently similar for you to be able to access another university system without much difficulty. But you will still find much that is unexpected and different, too. That is the appeal of Study Abroad and that is also the challenge.

Study Abroad not only enhances your understanding but broadens it, too, allowing you to cover topics which are not offered at home or which are presented abroad in a different way. Given the range and variety of modern scholarship, it is quite inevitable that the content of courses will differ in different countries. Even when the material covered is the same, the approach taken and the examples chosen to illustrate the subject will usually be different and are likely to relate partly to local circumstances. Therefore, you can develop your knowledge of your subject in many new areas. In addition, many students use Study Abroad as an opportunity to undertake research and are able to find materials locally to which they would not have had access at home. It all adds variety to spice up your studies.

Studying and learning

Another popular reason for studying abroad is to encounter new methods of teaching and learning. While there is no doubt that universities have a great deal in common, there are differences in how knowledge is transmitted and in how students learn in different countries. Appreciating different teaching styles and trying out different methods of learning are things you will already do at home. But abroad you can probably extend your range and choice significantly. By adding to your repertoire, you gain what are often called ‘transferable skills’, techniques you can apply in other academic contexts, once you return home.

Nearly everyone enjoys meeting students from another country. The fact that those you meet abroad share fewer of your received opinions than students at home always adds to the enjoyment. Some students say they choose to study abroad precisely because it allows them to hear diverse or unusual opinions – not all of them their own. Differences in the educational backgrounds of the students and in their national perspectives often make for lively exchanges, whatever the subject under discussion. When controversy palls, there is also interest in discovering that the search for knowledge in higher education is capable of uniting students with different backgrounds and views in a common, shared understanding.

Study Abroad and jobs

Another major motive for studying abroad is a much more practical one. What many students are looking for primarily is an enhancement of their job prospects. Study Abroad has a strong vocational appeal. Many jobs available to graduates today form part of the global economy. To be well suited for them, you are expected to be aware of different cultures, sensitive to their requirements, experienced in dealing with their peculiarities. Students who have studied abroad are uniquely well placed to fulfil those needs. They have shown themselves able to adjust to a new society, capable of becoming part of that society as a student, knowledgeable about its differences from their own and informed and expert on how to bridge those differences. These are assets to an employer operating in a global market, as an increasing number of enterprises now do.

Unfortunately, the evidence suggests that not all employers are aware of the fact. The employer's main market may be in a country very different from that in which you have studied and you may still have to make a case to convince them of your merits. As you are likely to have developed skills that can be applied in any area of intercultural communication, however, these can always be deployed initially on your employer and then diverted to the business in hand. Even if you intend to work at home in a purely local enterprise, your knowledge of what prevails in the wider world is likely to prove an asset. There is certainly no doubt that a c.v. is much enhanced by a reference to Study Abroad and by the insights and experiences gained thereby.

Studying 'abroad'

Study Abroad can also be pursued to understand better an entire community. People often feel drawn to a country other than their own, one they have perhaps read about or visited or come to know through relatives or friends. Becoming more familiar with this country or gaining a closer knowledge of its language and culture while studying there have an obvious appeal. Though student life has quite a lot in common whatever the country, studying abroad inevitably opens up contacts with a wider cross-section of local people and presents opportunities to interact with them, both within the institution and beyond it. Encountering differences in culture, customs, beliefs and practices is always a learning experience. With goodwill on your part (and some tolerance on theirs) such situations often become revealing and engrossing.

Those whose subject of study is another language or culture are quite often required (or will themselves choose) to spend a period in a country where that language is widely spoken and where that culture can be observed in every-day life. For them, the main reason to do so lies in the opportunities for personal observation and first-hand experience. All of them say that this direct contact transforms their classroom knowledge, giving them a depth of understanding not available from books alone. For students taking other subjects, these benefits are not as central to their studies but they are often crucial to their sense of becoming accepted and feeling part of another society, something which everyone abroad wants to experience.

Studying for yourself

At its simplest, Study Abroad students are often in search of a refreshing change of scene. Most students complete their entire education within one country. To study in another country offers you something more – a break from established routine and the challenge of coping with a different environment, not to mention a different language or accent. Many students who have studied abroad see the experience, however beneficial academically or vocationally, principally in terms of personal fulfilment. They feel it brings out new aspects of their personality. They often say that, after studying abroad, they feel more independent or more mature, more confident, more adaptable, more tolerant and more aware of their identity. Provided they haven't been too much in the sun, there is every reason to take their claims seriously.

Studying abroad also involves learning to see yourself as others see you. By appreciating the differences between one country and another, you come gradually to see your own country in a new light. You begin to realise how much you owe to your own cultural upbringing. This in turn gives you a different perspective on your own education system and enables you to see its strengths and weaknesses more clearly. This can be a revelation and it can be challenging, too. You may find yourself increasingly in sympathy with the poet who asked 'And what should they know of England, who only England know?' Scots certainly do!

Studying for fun and profit

When students meet to discuss their experiences of having studied abroad the conversation usually becomes lively and loud enough to disturb the neighbours. What is most keenly remembered is the sense of fun. Whereas study at home can seem earnest and sombre, the added need abroad to overcome new challenges and confront another culture can make it all seem – certainly in retrospect – distinctly entertaining and amusing. As the reminiscences pour forth, even scrapes and misadventures are recounted with fondness and humour.

If this is in part nostalgia, it gains something from the reality of returning home. In today's mass higher education environment, the student who has studied abroad stands out as someone different, someone willing to try something unusual, to confront the unfamiliar, to take more of a risk. It's a difference that communicates itself to everyone else, to your friends, fellow students, academic staff. It makes you more interesting to all of them (however loath they are to admit it) and marks you out as someone who can survive away from the herd.

WHO CAN STUDY ABROAD?

Study Abroad programmes in the United Kingdom are not open to everyone. Each institution decides individually what it can offer and to which of its students the offer applies. In some cases only students taking particular subjects or in a particular year of study are eligible. In others, what you can apply for may be limited to particular courses or tied to particular institutions abroad. Some areas of study, usually those with a very strictly defined set of domestic requirements, are likely to be excluded altogether.

Even when you are eligible, unless the Study Abroad element is a requirement of the degree, places are often in limited supply. This arises from the different programme structures. Most of them are exchanges, meaning that students move between two universities, one in the United Kingdom and one abroad, and numbers normally have to be kept in balance. As a result, getting a place may not be automatic even if you are qualified to apply, and programmes quite often involve a prior selection among applicants. To succeed can take both persistence and drive. A few programmes are purely discretionary – students can apply to go abroad and arrangements are made on an *ad hoc* and individual basis for each applicant. But those programmes must be approved by your university, and approval may not be straightforward. Yet, despite all the limitations, quite often some type of Study Abroad programme will be available for nearly everyone, sometimes postgraduates as well as undergraduates, and there will be a wide choice of where you can go and what you can study.

STUDY ABROAD AND QUALITY ASSURANCE

All Study Abroad programmes come within the operation of the systems of quality control in UK universities. As a result, your university will allow you to study abroad only at institutions which demonstrably operate quality standards similar to its own. The fact that many universities in other countries were founded by those who had studied abroad and often follow a curriculum similar to universities in the United Kingdom no doubt makes the recognition of overseas studies and qualifications easier. There has also long been an understanding that higher education in the world is inherently international and that, in consequence, experience of study in one country can quite often be substituted for experience required in another. But there need to be checks to ensure that the standards are comparable.

Each country has its own means of determining quality, and the process of deciding is not routine. It can relate, for example, to how staff are trained, to which courses are provided, to what methods of assessment are used, to the facilities provided or to the use of external monitoring. You should not expect the system that you encounter overseas to be identical to the one you know at home. Indeed, Study Abroad is attractive partly because it allows you to observe different structures and procedures. But you should feel confident that the supervision which is provided for you at home for you to undertake your studies successfully is the criterion which has been used to assess the supervision abroad. Without that, the exchange arrangement would not have been approved.

STUDY ABROAD AND STATUS

Study Abroad programmes are increasingly seen as evidence of an institution's international standing. A willingness to offer opportunities to study abroad is often taken as a sign that your university or college is outward looking, internationalist and progressive. Those who compile tables of university rankings (who are often at a loss to find objective criteria to distinguish one institution from another and who are, in consequence, particularly fond of statistics) have taken the data for Study Abroad as informatiom they can use. Some of the earliest ranking systems awarded institutions credit for their overseas numbers, rather like supermarket loyalty cards except in reverse: the points were awarded only if their customers shopped elsewhere.

Although the usefulness of university ranking tables is often questioned – indeed denied – the number of students studying abroad does seem genuinely to provide some evidence of vitality. It certainly suggests enterprise and initiative as both are involved in setting up such programmes. Of course, there may be other explanations for why students study abroad: it could even be the dubious nature of the local educational provision which is driving them out! But that cannot explain why those abroad are willing to come in exchange. Nor can it account for the fact that some students claim that the availability of a good Study Abroad programme is one of the factors they considered when selecting their university. If you have confidence in your choice of university, you can have equal confidence in the standing of its Study Abroad programmes.

SUPPORT FOR STUDY ABROAD: UNIVERSITIES

Support for studying abroad from universities and colleges is clear. Scholars have always wandered about the world in pursuit of knowledge and are no less eager to do so today, though their luggage is now weighed down with personal computers designed to allow them to communicate from home.

They are in general greatly pleased to find students following in their footsteps. They are aware that academic books today command a global readership, that academic conferences are increasingly international in membership and scope, that the staff of most major universities are drawn from many different countries, that funding for research comes often from international sources. Institutions boast of being enriched by all this. They also claim that having students drawn from different cultures and different educational systems makes them more inclusive, more cutting edge, more relevant to the needs of the modern world.

Over the last twenty years most colleges and universities have established International Offices or Study Abroad offices to support and encourage student mobility. Often they have also altered their rules and regulations to make it easier for students to count work done abroad as part of their degree. Many employ specialist staff, some from overseas, to assist those with questions concerning studying and living abroad. Some have created scholarships to help fund international study. Many have employment offices which provide advice on international jobs. The support is therefore clear, even if it is not incautious. Problems are usually outlined along with possibilities. But the days when students contemplating studying abroad felt like Odysseus venturing into the Unknown have long since gone.

SUPPORT FOR STUDY ABROAD: GOVERNMENTS

If you decide to study abroad, you can also be sure of strong support from the UK government. In recent years, it has even allocated resources and devoted personnel to ensure the success of some Study Abroad programmes. Of course, some see government support rather as Greeks bearing gifts were seen by the Spartans. But on this occasion there seems less reason for suspicion. Governments want to know that their students, who form part of the country's future generation of employers and employees, have the capacity to compete in the world economy. They are also aware of the importance of knowing your neighbour in a world where good neighbourliness brings diplomatic dividends. Since air travel makes everyone a neighbour, they hope that by encouraging Study Abroad they are also doing something to foster world-wide international understanding.

The government of the European Union is another example of this same approach. Its educational programmes explicitly support the idea that there is an added benefit when students are able to study in more than one country. Sometimes the goal of EU educational programmes is said to be the creation of a common European consciousness, ultimately allowing for a closer association of the countries of the European Union. Some political sceptics reach immediately for their rifles on hearing the word consciousness. But their concerns are usually assuaged on learning that there are also more immediate goals. It is hoped that by demonstrating to students the viability of working in more than one country, the EU educational programmes will eventually produce a freer, more mobile, more open job market for all its citizens.

STUDY ABROAD TODAY

Although Study Abroad opportunities have grown enormously, they are not available as widely as full degree studies. In general, most countries can accommodate international students in degree studies but many fewer provide special arrangements for visiting or occasional international students. For the United Kingdom, the principal programmes which operate are still those with North America and Europe. The United States was the earliest to develop Study Abroad programmes and the United Kingdom is still its principal partner. It also has more types of programme than any other country and these operate in many more countries. Some are even held at sea. The European Union has been involved in Study Abroad only since the 1970s. It has recently sought to extend its operation into Japan, China, India and beyond, but its main contribution is still within Europe and among EU countries. Australia and New Zealand have also become active, initially in response to US requests, though subsequently developing their own outreach and partnerships and sometimes their own approaches.

For much of the rest of the world, particularly Asia and Africa and Latin America, Study Abroad is still in its infancy. None the less, many individual institutions there have established successful programmes with partners overseas in other countries. There have also been several attempts at using other forms of association – Pan-Pacific, Commonwealth, Inter-African – to stimulate university contacts, and some successful programmes have emerged from that. These in turn have encouraged the formation of new programmes with institutions in the United Kingdom. Study Abroad in Britain is rapidly following the United States into these wider still and wider associations.

STUDYING ABROAD: THE PERILS

For all its considerable advantages, studying abroad is not without its perils although, thankfully, these are not encountered by everyone. For some, it can be disorienting. Those who have been doing outstandingly well in their studies at home are sometimes thrown by the differences between one education system and another and can underperform until they regain their balance. A few students get homesick while studying abroad and these feelings can affect their work. This can make the cultural adjustment which is required for Study Abroad overwhelming and a severe reaction against the host country can set in. There can also be extra costs involved, not simply in travel, but in the fact that you are less familiar with the locality and sometimes less able to live there economically. These costs can mount up, too.

When concerns like these become serious (something seldom experienced) the results can be critical. A small minority of students does encounter persistent academic problems;

some decide to break off studies and return home prematurely; and some feel that they have let themselves down by damagingly underestimating the difficulties involved. But you have to remember that academic and personal problems are just as likely – in some ways are even more likely – to occur at home. There is no evidence that studying abroad adds to them. Provided you are aware that things can go wrong and that, if they do, you will have to respond, there is no reason why you should not have confidence in your ability to cope.

SUMMARY

When asked to list the principal benefits of studying abroad, students suggest:

- Academic interest
- Learning skills
- Career prospects
- Wider knowledge
- Change of scene

Universities and governments add:

- Quality assurance
- Academic status
- International knowledge
- International understanding

The disadvantages are seen as:

- Unfamiliarity/homesickness
- Possible extra costs

SOME QUESTIONS

If you are interested in studying abroad, it is worth spending some time thinking out for yourself what issues you will have to confront. What for you are the advantages and disadvantages? What persuades you that you can cope with studying abroad? How does studying abroad fit into your degree course and into your future career plans? What is its main academic appeal and what, other than academic interest, would you hope to gain from it? How confident are you that you will get support for it from your family and friends?

3 THE MECHANICS

'It's a very different system here, initially very difficult to follow, but ultimately you see the benefits.'

'The exchange programme has fulfilled a demand from our students to extend their academic experience with a period of time abroad and has brought excellent students here from various countries, so benefiting the university community in general.'
(International Office information sheet)

To enable students to study abroad, universities and colleges have had to make a number of adjustments to their usual procedures. Earlier, studying abroad usually meant taking a 'year out' or involved you in taking extra time to complete your degree. It often meant doing a great deal of investigation to find out what was available and how you could benefit from this. It was not uncommon for students to have to continue to do work for their home university while abroad and for this work to be assessed on their return. The idea of allowing students to integrate completely into institutions abroad for up to a year meant a revolution in the way in which such studies were conducted. But, as with all revolutions, the new procedures often had their roots in the past. This chapter looks at how study abroad is currently arranged and outlines the ways in which, by studying abroad, you can contribute to your degree study at home.

STUDY RECOGNITION

Study Abroad makes use of a much older tradition in the United Kingdom of 'recognising' studies performed in universities abroad. Students who begin a degree in another country and are then obliged to move to Britain for personal or family reasons have long been allowed to transfer directly into a British university. In many cases, they are also allowed to count the studies done abroad as part of their degree requirements. Much depends, of course, on what they have already studied and what they wish to study in the United Kingdom. But it is often possible for them to begin, not in first year, but at a more advanced level and so to graduate more quickly.

Nowadays the process of recognising studies done elsewhere is usually known as 'assigning credit', which makes it sound as if enforcement by the bailiffs might be involved. But, though the use of a term more familiar in the world of commerce may be new, the procedure it describes is not. This follows exactly what has long been done for in-coming students and is simply a way of treating studies performed elsewhere as equivalent to studies at home. The key difference is in the timing. Whereas those transferring into the United Kingdom are given credit only after they have completed part of their overseas studies, for Study Abroad students credit has to be conferred provisionally in advance.

Course credits

There are, fundamentally, two aspects to the recognition of your studies abroad. The first is the 'credit' you are assigned. To obtain 'full credit' for your studies abroad, the programme of courses you take has to be regarded as equivalent in length, level of difficulty and appropriateness of content to what you would have done had you remained at home. Where you are following a full-year programme which roughly corresponds in length and content to what your fellow students are taking at home, this is generally easy, or easier, to assess. But, in choosing courses, you are likely to be bound by the same rules as students at your host institution and that can introduce some differences. It is not uncommon, for example, for the number of courses you have to take abroad to be different (sometimes fewer, sometimes more) or for specific requirements to have to be met which differ from those at home. You must just accept that in such matters some equivalents are more equivalent than others.

In order to obtain credit, you need to get approval from your own university, even before you begin your studies, for the programme and the courses you are taking abroad. This is likely to be a lengthy process, technical and bureaucratic, because university regulations are involved. It will probably involve the submission of an application (by you or on your behalf) to a central agency with the right to vet (and to question and amend) the proposals. But it may also be largely formal because the programme will already have received general approval and there will doubtless be many earlier precedents for what you are proposing to do. In fact, if everything is arranged for you, you may not even be aware that prior course approval is a requirement.

Course authorisation

In the legal phrase which is often used, your course of studies overseas is then recognised 'in lieu of', which means 'in place of', the studies you would otherwise have to take at home. This gives you the provisional authority to study abroad and acknowledges that the programme you are undertaking is regarded as equivalent to the one at home. Provided you pass, you can then be assured that these studies will count towards your degree once you return. Technically, this concession also exempts you from having to reside in the United Kingdom for the period you are away, which your degree regulations would otherwise normally require. In some cases (it is a requirement for the Erasmus programme – see p. 54), the whole arrangement is set out formally in what is called a Learning Agreement, which has to be approved by you, your university and your host university before you leave.

Course selection (the number, level and content as well as the choice) is always a crucial element in getting credit, and you are almost certainly going to need – and to be given – guidance from your own university here. Credit also requires that you must complete all the work of the course, which includes any regulations on attendance and on the submission of written work as well as completing the course overall. You clearly also have to follow whatever local students must do to satisfy the regulations. Finally, one of the more obvious and standard rules in Study Abroad is that those who fail or who do not complete the course will normally lose part or all of the course credit. That would presumably not be entirely different at home, whatever parents or the media allege.

Course harmonisation

When the courses you do while studying abroad are fully recognised, you can usually complete your degree in exactly the same time as if you had remained at home throughout. The only difficulty might be where the academic years differ and it is not possible to complete the overseas programme without extending the period of study. But that is unusual. Normally Study Abroad does fit into the academic year at home (even if in some cases it means doing semesters in reverse order or starting or finishing early) and the programmes generally run, like those in the United Kingdom, from autumn to the following summer.

The exact length of terms, semesters or academic years, however, can be different in different countries and, of course, you must complete the study period required abroad rather than the period you would have taken had you remained at home. In some cases, however, the period abroad for which you can apply will be less than a full year or a full semester, or the courses you have to take will not be those which local students take. If so, this will be clearly specified and you will probably be told what credit you are going to be allowed. Such matters will always have been discussed and settled in advance by the sending and receiving universities. All you need do is to find out what has been agreed.

Grades

The second element in credit recognition is what is called 'the grade'. This is simply the mark or level of attainment you have reached. It can be expressed as a number, a letter, a symbol or even words – different forms are used in different countries.

Usually, you are awarded marks for each assessed piece of work and an overall result is recorded for your entire course or programme, which is no doubt what you are familiar with already. But, for the grade to be credited to you at home, the assessments normally have to be 'translated' into whatever marking scale your own university uses. This translation is seldom automatic. Marking scales are quite commonly different in different countries, sometimes in different institutions, sometimes even within a single institution, and often bear little or no relation to one another. Some universities will despair at this, allow you a pass/fail grade and then refuse to convert further, on the grounds that exactitude in translating grades is beyond them.

They often have a point. If (as does happen) a university uses only three grades, good, pass and fail, the precise translation into, perhaps, a percentage scale is clearly not straightforward. In that case, the university with the economical marking scale is likely to be asked by its more profligate partners to communicate further information about each student's performance so that a closer approximation to a mark on a percentage scale can be achieved. Even percentage scales have their peculiarities, not least in that many institutions which employ them refuse to award marks above 70 per cent, presumably on the grounds that human beings require an ample latitude to acknowledge their fallibility. Others use the full ton. To ensure that common standards can be applied, whatever the peculiarities of local assessment practices, qualitative points of difference have to be established and agreed as assessment criteria between your home and your host university. These then need to be related to the two marking scales. Only once that is done can conversion tables be produced and published.

Grade equivalents

Wherever you are studying abroad, you should be told how the marks you get there are going to be rescaled for use at home when the grades are transferred. If you are not told, you should ask. For EU programmes, a new common scale has been devised, called the ECTS scale (European Credit Transfer Scheme), using numbers, bands of marks and verbal descriptions of what the marks mean. Everyone participating in EU programmes is expected to know this. It is intended that it should eventually evolve into a full credit accumulation system, permitting students to compare grades as easily between EU universities as between courses in the United Kingdom. Already, while marking scales in individual institutions throughout the EU remain various, grades have to be rescaled to fit the ECTS categories before being transmitted to the home institution – unless, of course, the host university has adopted the ECTS scale as its own.

Outside the European Union, there is not always a standard scale, though some see the GPA (Grade Point Average) system, used in the United States, as similar. This displays strong American common sense by generally using numbers, not the Greek letters and pluses and minuses once strongly favoured in traditional British institutions. But even GPA scales vary. Some use marks between 1 and 4, others 1 and 5, and some use multiples of 4. All allow for decimal points, some of which, in practice, can reach a degree of refinement which make the Greek letter grades look like models of restrained elegance. Whatever the case, the same advice applies. Where the scale differs from the one with which you are familiar, a conversion table will have to be employed, and that table is what you need to know.

Credit transfer

Assigning credit is one of the most complicated aspects of the process of studying abroad, as the history of ECTS shows. When initiating its Study Abroad programmes, the European Union tried initially to devise a common scale to be used everywhere for credits and grades. But, when the European Credit Transfer Scheme ultimately emerged, a different solution had triumphed. The organisers quickly discovered that it was impossible to demand exact parity between courses in different countries to determine credit. Each country has its own distinctive pattern of study, and courses tend to vary greatly in nature. They differ, for example, in the number of days or weeks over which they are taught, the number of units or individual course components included, the number of lectures delivered and practicals or tutorials held, the nature of work requirements, the elements of work to be assessed, and so on. To establish that a course of studies in one country is precisely equivalent to one in another proved to be virtually impossible. In the end, the European Union decided that it would have to operate 'by trust'.

Even within a single country, as in the United Kingdom, the differences in patterns of study between one institution and another are often marked. The lengths of terms in Oxford and Cambridge, for example, are not the same as those of most other UK institutions. The structure of semesters (a model derived only relatively recently from the United States) in those UK universities which employ them, currently displays some of the rich diversity and some of the boundless optimism of entries for the National Lottery. But, when there is widespread agreement that such differences are insignificant overall and merely reflect local preferences and needs, as seems to be the view about variations in course structures in the United Kingdom, then all is well. As in Mao's China, the thousand flowers can blossom and the thousand schools contend and harmony is held to emerge out of the tolerance of diversity.

Credit and trust

Being more prosaic and less Maoist, what operating 'by trust' means is allowing alternatives and permitting flexibility. It is acknowledged that there are differences between degree courses in different countries but everyone agrees that these should be treated as relatively unimportant. For example, what is held by the authorities in one country to be a full year's (or full semester's or full term's) programme has to be regarded by their partners in other countries as such. This is true even if there are significant variations in length or in how the programme is constructed from what obtains in partner institutions. Because the point of Study Abroad is to experience student life as a local, it is considered more important that you should do what all other students are doing locally rather than being required to duplicate precisely what you would have done at home. Study Abroad programmes in the United States had come to the same conclusion even earlier, and most had decided to give the same emphasis to trust.

There are, however, some limits to the flexibility which can be allowed. Some exchange partners have many things in common. In consequence, there will often be marked similarities between what you are familiar with from home and what you will be asked to do overseas. Others have programmes that are very different in content and make very different requirements. What you can be sure of is that the similarities and differences will have been considered by both sides and will be held to balance out overall. The intention is always to provide a comparable, and not necessarily identical, educational experience for those moving between one system and another. This is sometimes expressed by arguing that the two programmes, though not the same, enjoy a 'parity of esteem'.

DEGREE RECOGNITION

In recent years there have been various attempts by UK universities formally to recognise Study Abroad as forming part of the degree awarded. The problem is that degrees in the United Kingdom are individual to the universities that award them. Each sets its own standards (though these are moderated externally) and each alone decides if the standard has been reached. Your university can, if it chooses, acknowledge that studies performed elsewhere are comparable to those it provides. But, when it confers a degree on you, it has to do so in its own name. One way to give Study Abroad more recognition is for your university to supplement its degree award with a citation referring to the overseas experience. Degree awards take the form of a parchment, and a reference is sometimes made on that document to the period of Study Abroad. Alternatively, special additional forms can be added to the award for those students who undertake some of their studies abroad, so that these can be referred to or even copied to employers and other interested parties. European Union countries are gradually introducing Diploma Supplements for all bachelor and master awards. These will give a standardised EU-wide description of the content, nature and status of the award, so that they can be read and compared internationally. But Supplements are not yet universally an EU requirement, and they are still unusual elsewhere.

Some institutions have tried to go much further and, acting here very much in the spirit of EU regulations, make their award jointly with their partner institution. In this way, the student receives two qualifications, a degree from the home institution and some kind of award, perhaps a certificate, from the partner. Full double degrees, where both universities make the award, are already in existence, but mainly for a few postgraduate awards. They are less relevant for undergraduates where the study is overwhelmingly performed in only one institution. Earlier, the European Union proposed that students should eventually be able to move annually from one institution to another, each in a different country, and to claim their degree from whichever institution they attended last. If such a notion still sounds a long way off and rather fanciful for students seeking UK qualifications, there is no doubt that a willingness explicitly to recognise that degrees can and do now reflect study and teaching in more than one country is growing.

RESIDENCE REQUIREMENTS

British students, other than those on external programmes (that which would now often be called distance learning), have long had to reside throughout their period of studies within a reasonable distance of their university or college. The requirement seems to be intended to reflect many purposes. University life has always been seen as being more than just classroom learning, and no doubt a residence requirement ensured that students were brought into touch with each other and with their tutors when not in class. It may also be that a common residential rule ensured that students were attending classes or were at least in a position where they might be obliged to do so with a little spirited encouragement. Common residence also allowed the university authorities to know that they could rely on reaching all their students when they needed to do so. Study Abroad breaks with this tradition and so requires a different set of justifications.

The obvious one is that the students don't lose contact with tutors and fellow students when abroad but merely encounter a more diverse group of both. They become fully matriculated students in their partner institutions, as entitled to all the instruction and services provided there as any full-degree candidate. If the residential element which was earlier considered vital was that of building an academic community in which academic debate could flourish, then something extra is added when the community broadens out. If the key element is the fact that the university is *in loco parentis* and needs to be able to play that role, then a period of adoption, in which rights and responsibilities are transferred to another institution, preserves the intent. And, if what is important is that the university should remain in touch with those for whose education it has been created, then modern communications, e-mail, faxes, telephones, even rapid transport, ensure that this can be as readily and easily done from a distance as on site.

FINANCE

A mechanism has also emerged to overcome one of the major obstacles to studying abroad: its cost. In countries with a private educational system, the fee costs, directly charged to the student, can be considerable, which is one obstacle to exchanges. In those, like the United Kingdom, where education is largely funded by the state, the fees are usually smaller than in private institutions, but there is likely then to be a limit to the number of international students who can be accommodated. In some countries, again as in the United Kingdom, fees are low for local students but international students are charged a higher rate, which is another obstacle to mobility. Cost-of-living differentials between one country and another can add to the financial problems, unless you are lucky enough to be moving from a high-cost country to a low-cost one. Study Abroad, particularly outside the European Union, where other mechanisms can be used to hold down costs, has had to find a way round these difficulties.

One way of tackling them has been a resort to university-to-university agreements. Under most of these, students on each side are made liable only for whatever fees they would pay at home, the fees abroad being waived. Where that occurs, of course, the overseas fee charge ceases to be a significant issue. Some agreements, particularly those with North America, have even gone further and insisted that students on each side must also pay for a full-board accommodation place at their own institution, which they then exchange with their incoming partner. This effectively wipes out the cost-of-living differential, too, enabling students from lower-cost countries to move to higher-cost ones. Unfortunately, it does also mean that one set of students is paying more than they would have to, were they to be given direct access to the overseas institution. But some argue that the extra cost is compensated for by the high status enjoyed by the exchange students when abroad and by the guarantee, which they automatically have, of being allocated a place. Of course, arrangements vary between institutions and within institutions. Not all will make provision for this. All depends on the individual circumstances, which will no doubt be explained to you when you enquire.

SUMMARY

To enable students to count their studies abroad towards their degree at home, a mechanism has been devised which permits:

- Overseas study recognition
- Credit transfer
- Grade conversion and transfer
- Course equivalents
- Mutual fee waivers

These are dependent on:

- Appropriate course choice
- Approval at home and abroad
- The removal of residence requirements

SOME QUESTIONS

If you have decided that you would like to study abroad, do you know what arrangements your university has made for this? Can it be done without adding to the period for which you must study for your degree? Can you transfer back home not only course credits but grades? What agreements exist on the nature of the credits allowed? Are there agreements on fee payments and on other study costs? In tackling Study Abroad, are you going to meet encouragement or discouragement from your university or college?

4 EXCHANGES

'It was an awesome experience. It has given me direction and purpose and improved my language skills no end. And it will bring me back again after I finish my studies.'

'It was definitely worthwhile but I recommend really thinking about what you want when you choose where to go.'

Most UK students on Study Abroad programmes participate in exchanges. These are found in virtually every institution. They vary in scale from those catering to only one or two students up to those involving hundreds. Some are of considerable prestige and age. A few, particularly with the United States, have been operating for nearly half a century. Most are relatively recent and have yet to win – or perhaps to get – a reputation. Some are bilateral arrangements between a single college or university in the United Kingdom and overseas. Many are networks, involving perhaps dozens of partners in the United Kingdom and abroad. Yet, for all their diversity, they also have a good deal in common. This chapter looks at the kinds of programmes currently available and offers some advice on choosing the ones which would suit best.

HOW ARE EXCHANGES ARRANGED?

Exchanges can be arranged by third parties but are usually the outcome of an agreement between two institutions, one in the United Kingdom and one abroad. The primary purpose of the agreement is to allow students to move between one institution and the other for a period of up to an academic year. Agreements are also used to cement relations between the two signatories, and other forms of co-operation (staff exchanges and research collaboration, for example) are sometimes included in the terms. Signed on behalf of the whole institution, they can apply only to part of it (a department or area of studies) or to a particular group of students (second-year undergraduates taking international business degrees, for example).

The agreements are often also used to set out the terms under which the exchange of students takes place. Typically, this includes the understanding that neither institution will levy tuition fees on students from the other. Commonly, there are also clauses on accommodation and welfare provision, usually explaining what students can expect or can't expect in these respects, and some reference to the fact that each side will regard the other's students as entitled to all the privileges, rights and responsibilities enjoyed by their own. There are also likely to be clauses on the maximum numbers who can be accommodated on the exchange and on any entry conditions which either side wishes to apply (minimum language requirements, for example).

WHICH STUDENTS CAN APPLY?

To apply for an exchange, you obviously have to be within the categories specified in the agreements, though it is always worth enquiring to see if there is any flexibility in what can be allowed. If there is an exchange which applies to you, you are likely to hear about it from your lecturers or tutors or perhaps from the central administrative office in the university which has been given the job of looking after exchanges. You may even have first heard about it when applying to university, since many institutions now use their Study Abroad programmes as an aspect of their recruitment strategy. If so, the information will certainly be repeated somewhere once your turn to apply comes around. The difficulty is to know exactly where. It might be sensible to let someone in authority know that you are interested (your academic adviser?) just to make sure that you are kept informed and can apply in good time.

Obviously, if the study abroad is compulsory and an exchange place is available for everyone, then you simply have to be qualified to enter that stage of your course. In many cases, this will require more than a simple pass, but that is a matter for each individual subject area and each individual institution. Unfortunately, if the study abroad is not compulsory, it is seldom enough to come within the categories specified in order to gain a place. Most exchanges are quite popular and rather competitive. There will usually be a defined number of places and you will probably have to throw your hat in the ring and hope that it is fetching enough to get you noticed.

WHY CHOOSE AN EXCHANGE?

Participating in an exchange offers you clear advantages over other forms of studying abroad. You may have to be chosen by your home institution but you don't normally have to undergo any selection process abroad. You normally pay no course fees to the host institution and, if your fees are paid for you at home by government, this continues when you are abroad. You are often given privileged access to courses and study opportunities in your host institution, at least to the extent of being treated equally with local senior students. Your status as a guest from a partner institution can open doors for you. And you will have the guarantee, provided only that you have followed instructions, that the courses you do and the grades you obtain will enable you to progress with your studies at home almost automatically.

You are also likely to be better informed than other students abroad about what you are taking on. It is usually possible to discuss the prospects with students from your host institution before you go. If the exchange has lasted for a few years, some of them will be currently studying at your university and some of your own fellow degree students will have returned from there, too. This contact allows you to feel more confident about the whole process. You have the security, too, which comes from knowing that, if anything untoward arises, you can refer the matter back to your own university and get advice and assistance. After all, you are still a student there and entitled to its support, and it is responsible for the exchange and so for ensuring that everything operates smoothly.

SELECTING AN EXCHANGE

Your university will probably offer you a choice of more than one exchange programme, and you will almost always have a choice of courses. That is no doubt welcome but making the selection of a country, institution or course at a distance is not always easy and will require some care. Fortunately, because exchanges are all official and the staff on both sides often know each other personally, there is usually a large amount of information about each exchange destination which you can obtain from within your institution and often a good deal of help in interpreting what you read. You should first arm yourself with a list of possible countries and possible institutions, and then try to find out as much as you can about all of them or at least the ones that look most appealing. The advice you get from the exchange officials will be hugely helpful but you should remember that they will regard all their programmes as worthy (probably equally worthy) and may expect you to have your own views on how the selection is to be made.

Making a choice usually involves thinking about yourself as an individual and what most attracts you to studying abroad. You will find that you first have to decide what you like and don't like about your studies more generally, and then you have to try to relate your preferences to what is on offer. In some ways, it is a little like computer dating – though with fewer risks of embarrassment. It also helps that you, and not the computers, have to arrange the pairings. Most people faced with a choice begin by looking at their individual situations, personality, interests, experience, career plans and future prospects. It also helps if you know generally what you are hoping most to gain from the period abroad and what, if anything, you are keen to avoid.

SELECTING A COUNTRY: THE UNITED STATES AND THE EUROPEAN UNION

When you have a choice of countries, this has to be settled first. Most United Kingdom exchanges are either with the United States or with the European Union. Both have hugely prestigious educational institutions; and both have enormous appeal as Study Abroad destinations. The greatest attraction of the United States for most British students is its language of instruction – English. But it also offers an almost unrivalled range of institutions in a vast country with markedly different regional identities. American education is also well known in the United Kingdom and very highly regarded. The division between public and private institutions, which is much less familiar in Britain, is usually seen as an additional attraction.

The main appeal of the European Union is its geographic closeness to the United Kingdom and the fact that it consists of countries working together in an association of which Britain is a member. Political and vocational reasons, therefore, suggest the choice. Within the European Union, too, you will find a remarkably diverse educational provision and a striking variety of different cultures and environments from which to choose. Those with the requisite language skills or the desire to acquire them will be attracted for that reason, too, and help in learning languages is often provided as part of these programmes. Of course, there are people who maintain that it is easier to be understood using English on the European continent than in the United States. But that is not something on which you should base your choice.

SELECTING A COUNTRY: THE WIDER WORLD

The range of countries which you can consider extends worldwide. All the countries of the Commonwealth have educational systems which share a good deal with what is found in the United Kingdom. In their diversity of educational provision, their use of English and in the depth of their contacts with Britain, they offer opportunities for study which are at once accessible and distinctive. The countries of East Asia, by contrast, do require some necessary language skills but also offer fascinating, contrasting experiences. Japan, for example, has a tradition of popular education and a current generosity of higher education provision almost equalling the United States. China boasts a very different, highly selective, educational tradition, one of the greatest antiquity, which is rapidly being transformed into something dynamic and contemporary.

The countries of south-east Asia, the Middle East, Latin America and Africa, where Study Abroad is much less developed, also have their own powerful educational appeal. Although never large in terms of numbers involved, they are often the first choice of many in development studies or politics or business. Experiencing something very different to the familiar educational systems of the west is often the main reason for selecting them. Whatever your interests and wherever you search, there are going to be several possibilities. If the whole world is your oyster, there's no telling where the pearls may be found.

DECIDING ON AN EXCHANGE COUNTRY

Fortunately, most of us don't begin by considering the entire planet. We immediately narrow the choice down to those countries which we believe would suit us best. That focus is likely to result from several considerations, some of which will be entirely personal. More generally, the reputation of the country in the studies you want to undertake is often one major consideration. That is an area where your tutors can usually offer a reliable opinion. The popularity of the particular exchanges is another frequently used test. One way to judge that is by the numbers who apply – though knowing that the competition will be tough may put you off. The strength of the local educational system, so far as you understand it, is sometimes used as a gauge for how secure you might feel there. But it is true that many of the world's higher educational systems inspire a good deal of confidence. Any that don't are likely to be considered only by those with other reasons for choosing them.

The supports you can hope to have in that country are also matters which can be of importance but that can be highly personal to you. The possibility of a working environment compatible with your own preferences is a more precise and, therefore, a more easily verifiable consideration. Again, tutors should be able to provide the facts. A sense of having met with reliable service in a country you have come to know can influence your decision. Feeling a personal affinity for a particular country, for whatever reason, seems to be behind many of the choices made. Being offered advice in making your selection by someone whom you respect is another powerful inducement. There is no one way of making the decision. Many things contribute to it.

PRACTICAL CONSIDERATIONS

Where financial issues loom large for you, you may also have to give thought to such matters as the cost of travel, the local cost of living, the possibility of being able to find work and to earn while studying (or before or after studying). Where issues of personal safety or health considerations are uppermost, you may want reassurance on those. If you are a student of the humanities, you may want to be where good cultural resources are on hand. If a scientist, you may want access to particular facilities. The possibility of being able to combine your studies with other activities, visits, experiences, may be something you see as important. Programme advisers can generally answer questions on all these matters or can refer them back to the partner institution to obtain the information you seek. Eventually, by combining country appraisal with self-examination, some preferences will begin to emerge.

If you are going to study abroad successfully, you have at least to begin with the belief that what you are taking on looks promising and presents no obvious disincentives. There is little point in persisting if you feel frustrated at every turn. With exchanges, it is easy to ask for reassurance and normally the answers you are given are carefully balanced and fair. With usually no pressure to find sufficient recruits, the home and host universities are likely to be much more concerned with placing you accurately rather than persuading you to fill a vacant slot. But you can always appear cynical to keep them on their toes.

SELECTING AN EXCHANGE INSTITUTION

Unless you find that you have no choice, selecting an institution is likely to be even more taxing than deciding on a country. Quite often you are faced – on a much smaller scale – with a choice similar to the one you had to make when you first decided to go to university. You are confronted with several possible institutions, all of which claim to be the best thing since the Beatles' *Revolver* album. Once more, you may have to resort to considering such matters as geographical location (are they city centre, suburban, rural or campus based?). Or you may want to make your decisions on grounds of academic prestige (though reputation is likely to be as hotly debated abroad as it is in the United Kingdom, and exchanges all tend usually to take place with institutions of similar standing to your own). The size of the institution may matter to you, or its facilities for students. You are again going to have to think about matching your preferences or tailoring your interests to the prospects offered.

Deciding such matters at a distance is the unfamiliar element. You are unlikely to be able to visit and inspect any of the universities to enable you to make up your mind. But the problem is not as large as first appears. Although you cannot get a sense of the atmosphere for yourself, you can be sure that others will have done this on your behalf. Your university's support for the exchange is a guarantee that it should be able to answer your questions on this as on any other relevant issue. In choosing among exchange options, you can also be confident that all of them have something to offer. What you are faced with, if there is a choice, is not the need to eliminate the unsuitable (that has already been done on your behalf) but simply to decide which would work best for you.

SELECTING A PROGRAMME

If the exchange is a compulsory element of your degree, it is certain that the partner institutions will have been chosen because of their strength in your area of studies. When exchanges are optional and open to students across the institution, you may have to give some thought to how far the ones you are considering fit with your particular subject interests. There are clear differences here between one university and another. The search may involve you in some work to discover the range of courses on offer in your subject area and even more to discover the names and expertise of the staff who teach there, though both of these may be important to you. But there is an easy short cut on offer. You can ask some members of staff in your own department what reputation they think the exchange institution has.

If you are sure that the exchange offers strength in your subject or area of studies, what other factors might be important? You may want to find out about how the subject is taught, about the approaches taken and the kinds of tasks which students are asked to perform. This is not to suggest that you should choose only the model with which you are most familiar. One of the advantages of Study Abroad is that it gives you the chance to try out alternatives. But you do have to know that the alternative attracts. You may want to delve into new areas of your subject or to tackle new subjects, so your investigation may have to be wide enough to include areas of study outside your own. This all takes time and effort and seems a bit much when you haven't yet got a place. But how else are you to feel confident about your choice?

COURSE SELECTION

In some cases, when the study abroad is compulsory, for example, your choice of courses abroad may be limited and defined. Particularly with department-to-department exchanges, the whole programme may be prescribed and you may be confined to a single set of courses within a single field of studies. This is presumably not essentially different from what you would encounter at home. Even in those circumstances, however, you should expect to have an element of choice. In other cases, when the study is optional, your choice may be very wide indeed. But, to obtain full credit, what you select at the host institution, as at home, will probably be subject to some limitations. If so, the intention is always to ensure that what you choose fits better into your programme at home, allowing you to resume your studies on your return without difficulty.

In the United Kingdom, after first year, you are usually doing some work at an advanced level. There are also sometimes specific subject requirements that must be completed. If so, it is possible that your university will insist that, when you are abroad, you must choose similarly advanced-level courses even if this is not a restriction imposed on local students. You may also have to find close alternatives to subject requirements you would have been expected to follow at home. What is important is that you should know if such restrictions exist and then make your choices in that light. Most universities have libraries or resource centres which contain copies of the prospectuses and study materials for exchange universities. The information is also likely to be available on the Internet, though you may need to hunt out the website addresses.

If, when it comes to course selection, you feel that the official prospectus is a poor substitute for the unofficial student jungle telegraph, you can then turn to the students in your institution from your partner university. If you don't know any or if they have all returned, you can ask to be put in e-mail contact with them.

EXERCISING CHOICE

Most Study Abroad programmes, even those where your choice is generally quite restricted, have some flexibility. It is recognised that your reasons for studying abroad can relate to a wish to acquire knowledge of some subject not readily obtainable at home. In that case, a modification of your programme may be possible to allow you to seize the opportunity which has arisen. If you are particularly keen while abroad to tackle some subject not normally included in your curriculum, then make your wishes known to your home advisers and ask for the matter to be considered. There must, however, always be some tension between flexibility and the need to keep on track with your studies at home. Invariably to insist on skiing off-*piste* when conditions are difficult can mean coming home with your leg in plaster.

On the other hand, being able to tackle programmes which look unorthodox or unusual may be one of the real benefits you get from being abroad. Some universities, for example, offer courses which are very different from traditional United Kingdom lecture courses but may be no less valuable or interesting. There may be ones, for example, which require individual projects and offer personal supervision and which have no formal classes at all. Others may concentrate on providing you with a kind of research experience within a group, rather than a lecture course. Not being willing to tackle a programme simply because it imperfectly resembles what you are used to from home may be as myopic as always insisting that everything must be different. Making a choice can require flexibility from you, too.

EXCHANGES AND ADMINISTRATION

Because your university is responsible for its exchanges, it will certainly do a great deal to ensure that they work well. The international administrative staff of the university will be available before, during and after your study abroad to help you deal with any problems which arise. This assistance can be very extensive, if you require it. It usually starts before you apply, continues while you are making your application, includes external matters, such as help in obtaining immigration documents where necessary, and may even cover advice on travel and living abroad.

To benefit from it fully you will need to make and retain a list of contact and e-mail addresses, for immediate use and for use once you are abroad. Finding out to whom to refer (and for what) has to be done before you leave. This includes administrative staff working on the programme and academic and advisory staff in your own department. You may often have to use this list when you are abroad to sort out matters which arise, including making decisions about your future, such as choosing the courses you will take on your return. It is simple to do things at a distance if you have got all the necessary contact details with you, and it can be complex if you have not. Though your contact people will be busy, it is also a good idea for you to think of keeping some of them in the picture while you are abroad, not only when you require their help but also when you feel things are going well. They will then assume that you are keen to share your pleasure with them, which is certain to earn you generous brownie points.

ONE-WAY EXCHANGES

Not all Study Abroad programmes are, in fact, real exchanges. Some, usually a small number, are arranged so as to allow students to move in only one direction. These are sometimes called 'one-way exchanges', presumably an analogy with the famous Zen notion of 'one-hand clapping'. They do resemble bilateral exchanges in many respects. For example, they are usually based on an agreement signed between the two institutions. Students normally apply through their own university. Again, you have to be selected by your own university to participate, and you will be subject to its rules on what you should study. Application is likely to be made through your own university, and it may also make arrangements for you to be allocated accommodation and board in the host institution. It is also possible that you will be liable for fees at your own university but not at the university you are visiting. These arrangements are more common with students coming into the United Kingdom from abroad rather than with those going in the opposite direction but you may still encounter examples or variants of them.

In other cases, one-way exchanges resemble independent study more than bilateral exchanges. Some students on one-way exchanges, for example, do pay fees directly to the host institution and not to the home one. Some are expected to apply abroad directly to the partner institution and may have the freedom to choose what they will study, though this is usually on the understanding that credit will have to be negotiated in advance with their university at home. The principal difference from independent study is simply that a special arrangement has been set up between the two institutions involved. This is designed to make it clear that it is not you as an individual but your university that is sponsoring the study abroad. The intention is to try to create more of a bilateral, university-to-university basis for the programme. This is seen as adding prestige and status to the arrangement by conferring on it something of a special relationship between two institutions.

SUMMARY

The rules governing exchanges generally include:

- Specific university 'partners'
- Defined student eligibility

- Privileged status
- Country choice
- Institutional choice
- Course choice
- Central supervision/assistance

SOME QUESTIONS

Is exchange the best way for you to study abroad? What particularly appeals to you about it? What do you think are its drawbacks? Does the choice of countries and institutions available to you have a real appeal? Are there going to be problems in reconciling the curriculum you have to follow to make progress with your degree and the choice which is available to you in your exchange institution?

5 STUDYING ABROAD OUTSIDE EXCHANGES

'It is worth getting on an exchange if you can. But it's not the end of the world if you don't.'

'It is easy to get forgotten about when you're abroad.'

Not all students on Study Abroad go on exchanges. Some, though a very much smaller number, also undertake Study Abroad independently. Once this was the most common form of studying abroad and, even if it long since lost that position, it still has a following. Studying independently is sometimes regarded as more interesting or more exciting than studying on formal exchanges. Many universities, too, are willing to accept that independent study does have a place. If you have set your heart on studying in some particular country where there is no exchange available or where the exchanges available are not open to you, it may be possible to negotiate your own arrangements. It is never a simple option and no one should take it on who is not determined, industrious and hugely energetic. But, if you are all of those things, this chapter contains some hints on how you might proceed.

INDEPENDENT STUDY

The mechanics of credit transfer do make it possible, theoretically, for you to study anywhere in the world, provided only that the institution you choose is a 'recognised' one. The same rules governing the recognition of studies which apply to incoming students clearly can apply to outgoing ones as well. Once more, if you had begun studying in any overseas institution and then moved to the United Kingdom, you would be in a position to ask for 'credit'. In consequence, on analogy with the rules which govern exchanges, it may be possible for you to request provisional credit in advance if you intend to study anywhere else. This is not, of course, to say in either case that you must necessarily be successful. Credit is a matter for your university to decide. It may be refused – it quite often is – and all the usual caveats about the need to have comparable subjects, content and standards in order to claim credit again operate.

If you are allowed to study abroad in an institution of your choice, your university can also allow you to count that study towards your degree. Clearly there needs to be prior agreement about where you will go and what you will study, just as there is on a recognised exchange. The normal requirement is that the institution you choose must have a status and reputation which inspire confidence (though a great many do) and you must be able to find courses there which would advance your knowledge and help you make progress in your discipline. If all that is satisfactorily established, and if all other barriers to entry are surmounted (both important conditions), you may even be permitted to regard your time there as equivalent to time spent in your home institution, just as exchange students do.

Quality issues

But there are problems in studying independently which must be considered. Firstly, in setting up an exchange, your university takes a great many factors into consideration other than the courses the students will take. It will almost certainly check, for example, that its partner is guided by professional standards which are similar to those it uses itself. This will apply to such detailed matters as the qualifications of staff, the levels at which academic standards are set, the facilities available to students, the means of ensuring that courses are properly approved and assessed, even the ratio of staff to students.

Obviously, no such checks will have been carried out where the study you are proposing to take is in an institution that is not an exchange partner. All that is usually considered for students on transfer from 'recognised institutions' is that the course must be of comparable standard and with comparable content. When this is not immediately clear, applicants are sometimes interviewed and examined and the facts established before the credit is allowed. There is therefore a danger for your university in allowing you to take a course for graduation unless it can make the checks which it has to make for exchanges. That can mean doing as much work for one individual as is required to service an entire exchange. In consequence, some universities, particularly those with a strong exchange programme of their own, will simply refuse to allow you to study for credit in a non-exchange institution.

Practical issues

Secondly, if a programme is to be arranged independently, your university will probably expect you to do most of the work in setting this up. They will expect you to establish that your preferred overseas institution is willing to accommodate you. They will also expect you to convince the authorities in your own department or in the university more widely that the studies you propose to undertake are comparable to those available at home. This means that you have to obtain copies of prospectuses, degree regulations and detailed course information, and then submit those for inspection, initially within your own department. It takes a good deal of time for this to be done and even more for the department to consider the matter and give its verdict.

You may be lucky. There may be someone in your area of studies who knows where you want to study and is willing to help you get there. There may be an International Office or a Study Abroad office which is able to guide you towards helpful sources of information and advice. Even so, you must be cautious. Universities throughout the world are alike in many ways but they are also different and individual, and their circumstances can change quite dramatically. If they are suddenly starved of funds or involved in some political crisis, even once-reputable places may become problematic. Before you commit yourself to studying anywhere independently, you need up-to-date information and some contemporary insights from those who know the place at first hand.

Loyalties

Thirdly, there is the problem of loyalties. If your university has set up exchanges with particular universities in particular countries, it may not be delighted to learn that you are not much attracted by them. It will probably feel that it has researched the field to decide which would be best for its students and made its selection accordingly. To learn that this selection is inadequate in your eyes may not be well received. There may even be a suspicion that you are uncertain of winning a place on the exchanges and so are trying to get round the competition.

Your university may feel it can offer a better solution. If it is sure that you would make a good exchange student and that no place is available for you, it may be able to use its contacts with its partner institutions to arrange something for you. Often, where exchanges apply only in one particular area of studies, both parties are willing to consider those from other areas when deserving cases arise. If that is so, it may be possible to get an exemption from the terms of the agreement in order to allow you to participate. An agreement can also be extended temporarily into new areas (to include postgraduates as well as undergraduates, for example). On the whole, that tends to be a more secure method of studying abroad than branching out on your own, and it may be much more welcome to your university. It is certainly worth enquiring about possibilities.

Financial issues

The biggest problem of independent study is cost. The mechanics of exchanges are designed to ensure financial viability for students on both sides. If you go on your own, you will probably be subject to greatly increased costs. You may remain liable for any fees you pay at home and also be liable for the fees at your host university. The fees abroad may be higher than local students pay since there has been a general move into commercial international education throughout the world. There can be extra charges, too, for examinations, for field trips and for welfare facilities. Given also questions of travel costs and living costs, you may find that the whole business is becoming quite uneconomical.

Or you may not. Some universities, when they feel enthusiastic about independent study, are willing to go the extra mile with you. A few will arrange matters so that you are not charged the full fee at home, though they may still claim part. This may seem to some institutions a reasonable enough concession, after all, since, if you are abroad, you won't be gaining much direct benefit from the instruction provided at home. Some are prepared to state to your local or national education authority in advance that they will recognise your studies overseas, which can be enough to bring them round in support, too. That may even mean that you can hope for some financial assistance in studying abroad. But financial support for independent study is certainly not something on which you can rely, and you must make your enquiries long before your final decision is made. Most local authorities, for example, have explicit rules against assisting anyone, outside exchanges, whose overseas programme is not recognised as a compulsory element of their course.

Value for money

When you have to pay tuition fees, you become aware immediately of the vast range of costs world-wide and the difficulty of making comparisons. Within a single country, such as in the United States, there may be costs which range from sums below what is charged in Britain up to those which are many, many times larger. It is seldom enough simply to know the tuition charge. What you have to know is what you get for your money. Prestigious institutions which charge more are usually selling a great deal more than their prestige. They may provide more individual instruction, for example, or they may have a better record of achieving high results for their students or they may offer extras, such as accommodation or meal plans on an inclusive or non-commercial basis. Some may have particularly high-quality services, libraries, sports facilities, welfare provision.

On the other hand, the cost of tuition is likely to reflect in part the local cost of living, unless the government is offering subsidies. This means that fees in high-cost countries tend to be much larger than those elsewhere, almost irrespective of the quality of the product. If you are searching for value for money, as independent students usually are, you may have to cast your net widely. You may also have to get behind the ballpark figures to decide, using the popular American vernacular, what bang you are getting for your bucks.

Leaves of absence

Finally, if all the strategies of working through your own institution fail, you have the option of simply withdrawing from your studies for a time in order to undertake independent studies. Most universities do allow students to apply for a 'leave of absence', though they generally expect you to produce some good reasons for requesting it. If you are allowed leave and your wish to study elsewhere for a time is accepted as a valid reason for applying, then you can begin to plan. You are roughly in the position of someone taking a gap year but in the middle, rather than before the start, of your degree. Once granted permission, you are free to choose where to go and what to do.

You still have to remember, of course, that not all overseas institutions can accommodate students on 'occasional' studies.

You may also find that, because you are on leave, some universities abroad will be suspicious and will tell you that only those with a degree qualification can be considered for entry. To counteract this, it might be best to obtain from the Registry a partial transcript (there may be a small charge for this), setting out the courses you have taken and the grades you have obtained thus far, and you may need references from some of your tutors. A letter from someone in authority certifying that you are still a student in good standing would also be useful in any application you make.

Leave: the consequences

There are, of course, serious cost implications in travelling abroad to study on your own. Not only do you face all the usual costs (travel, tuition fees, local living expenses), but you are also lengthening your period of study. None of your studies abroad will count towards your degree. That is the most serious consequence of seeking the leave of absence. You will therefore also have to find the means for a whole extra year of study.

Nor is that the only difficulty. Problems can arise when you get out of step with what in India are called your 'batchmates'. Courses change in content from year to year. New approaches are introduced. The teaching staff changes. This can make it harder for you when you return home after your year 'out' to complete the studies for your degree. Remaining a student for an extra year may also require more stamina and commitment than you first realised. Though many people say that student days are the happiest days of your life, it can be difficult to sustain interest in them when they are unduly prolonged. Taking a leave of absence is probably best seen only as a final resort. If all else has failed except your passion to achieve your goal, then it may still have a place.

The prospects

None the less, if you are determined to study independently and if your studies are recognised, a year abroad in which you choose your own destination and make your own arrangements is often a rewarding one. In particular, you can choose to go to those institutions that have the most interest for you rather than the ones which your university sees as a match for itself. Most students who take up this opportunity have strong reasons for doing so – they have often lived before in the country of their choice or they have family who live there or they have become closely attached to it through their studies. In general, their motivation is extremely high and this is often a crucial element in ensuring that they are successful.

The one essential point is to remember to keep in close touch with your university at home. As someone outside the normal study arrangements, you are quite likely to be overlooked. Many matters which bear on your studies after you return will doubtless be discussed while you are away. You therefore need to ensure that someone at home is aware of where you have gone and what you are doing and is periodically reminded that you will be returning at the end of the year. It might help to correspond with someone on the teaching staff and with a fellow student because the information you need may come from both quarters. With such support, your independent study may avoid some of the problems often encountered and prove viable and rewarding.

SUMMARY

Independent study is possible but requires attention to:

- Gaining home university approval
- Quality considerations

- Applying individually
- The extra costs
- Considering a leave of absence

SOME QUESTIONS

If you want to study privately, do you know what arrangements your university will allow? Do you know where you want to go sufficiently well to be able to make the arrangements yourself? Have you thought through all the consequences, particularly those relating to funding?

6 THE EUROPEAN PROGRAMMES

'It was wicked. I just didn't want to come back.'

'It was very interesting to be integrated into a completely different education system, although very challenging at times.'

To round off this survey of Study Abroad opportunities, the next two chapters look in detail at the principal destinations for students from the United Kingdom, namely, the European Union and the United States of America. Many students who participate in them have little knowledge of EU study programmes. This chapter provides a brief sketch of their history and outlines a few issues currently in debate. As the focus is on the United Kingdom, it may serve as a talking point for those who go on these exchanges. It may also alert those with an interest to the number of programmes now involved, which seems to grow almost by the hour.

PARTICIPANTS

The main thrust of European Union educational programmes has always been an attempt to foster mobility among member countries, and students have always been at the heart of it. With the growth in size of the organisation, the outreach of the programmes has also extended. Today thirty-one countries take part in Socrates/Erasmus (see pp. 56–7). These include the twenty-five member states (Austria, Belgium, Denmark, Finland, France, Germany, Greece, Ireland, Italy, Luxembourg, Netherlands, Portugal, Spain, Sweden, United Kingdom, Cyprus, Czech Republic, Estonia, Hungary, Lithuania, Latvia,

Malta, Poland, Slovenia and Slovak Republic), three European Economic Area countries (Iceland, Liechtenstein and Norway) and three candidate countries (Bulgaria, Romania and Turkey). Switzerland has a kind of associated status. Around two thousand higher-educational institutions in total currently participate.

Not all, however, participate equally. At present, the principal receiving country is Spain, and the principal sending ones are France, Germany, Spain and Italy. Countries with smaller populations have, of course, fewer participants, though this is not necessarily true relatively. In fact, many countries with languages in less common use outside their own borders, like Greece or the Czech Republic, are particularly active in sending students abroad. In some ways, this is surprising. The programmes are meant to be mutual exchanges and it was feared that a failure of demand for inward mobility would necessarily constrain outward mobility, too. None the less, the picture of varied participation is likely to be reflected in what your own institution will offer.

ERASMUS

Socrates/Erasmus is the name usually given to the principal programme to promote international student mobility and student exchange within the European Union. It is now by far the most popular single exchange scheme in the United Kingdom. Its alternative names, however, reflect a controversial history. When initiated in 1987, the programme was called ERASMUS, partly as an acronym (it was supposed to have represented 'the European Community action scheme for the mobility of university students'), partly to honour the celebrated early-Renaissance Dutch philosopher, humanist and theologian of that name, a contemporary and close friend of Sir Thomas More (1478–1535). Erasmus (1466?–1536) dedicated his classic text, *In Praise of Folly*, to More though that was not the work, one assumes, in the minds of those who chose his name.

As first set up, ERASMUS owed something to the old notion of educational filtration, whereby scarce resources are channelled to an élite (in this case, university students) seen as the providers of society's future opinion formers and teachers. The assumption was that this would ensure that the knowledge and experience generated would drip down to everyone else eventually, too. But, though the ERASMUS programme was undoubtedly a popular success, it had its critics. Funding was limited and, as time passed, the élitist nature of the project was questioned, particularly as the benefits seemed to go disproportionately to the mobile students who were never more than 5 per cent of the total in higher education. It also became clear that those outside higher-educational institutions might need to gain more direct benefits if they were to give their enthusiastic support.

SOCRATES

In 1995, the programme was relaunched, with enlarged and assured funding, as Socrates, named in honour of another European scholar and pedagogue (Socrates [469?–399 BC] the Athenian philosopher). As a title, this was a backward leap historically but, in most other respects, constituted a definite step forward. Socrates extended in reach far beyond its predecessor. Its latest manifestation is Socrates II (to avoid linguistic favouritism among member nations, the European Union has employed a name from Ancient Greece and a numeral from Ancient Rome). This tries to offer some support for European educational ventures for everyone from school children to doctoral students, teachers to adult learners and both virtual and actual mobility programmes. Yet Erasmus, as a central component, survives still, now as the higher-educational arm of Socrates.

Under changes outlined for the period after 2006, Socrates, like Erasmus earlier, will be subsumed within a broader framework and will presumably bear yet another name. But the future direction is already clear. The European Union is now trying to promote lifelong learning for all. Its educational support and programmes will extend from cradle to grave, or at least from school learning to continuing professional development. In practice, however, financial constraints limit what it can try to achieve and, despite the planned changes, it has not lost its faith in the capacity of higher education to produce the teachers and disseminators of the knowledge and skills that it favours. Higher-education mobility schemes, in their various forms, will remain central elements in the entire programme for the foreseeable future.

SOCRATES/ERASMUS

The Socrates/Erasmus programme is managed by the European Commission and based in Brussels. Centrally regulated, the administration is devolved on to national bodies and they, in turn, devolve much on to the individual institutions. This is where the key decisions are made and where you are likely to hear first of Socrates/Erasmus opportunities for you. Under the programme, you have the chance to study for up to a year in any other member state or in those European countries outside the European Union which are participants. The intention primarily is to benefit citizens of the Union, but non-EU citizens, if studying in the EU, can also often take part. You are not likely to find that your own institution will have partners in all thirty-one participating countries but a variety of partners in a range of countries is the norm. Given Europe's varied and extensive higher-education provision and given its reputation (its universities and colleges include many of the earliest foundations and are among the best known in the world), the programme's success has been assured.

Socrates/Erasmus operates through exchanges which are proposed initially by institutional partners and implemented once endorsed centrally. The diversity of subjects and approaches on offer is a characteristic, as are programmes which meet particular, specific strategic goals. In recent years, for example, there has been a stress on the need for exchanges to be able to demonstrate benefits for a wider group of students within an institution rather than simply those participating in the exchange. This has meant favouring some which foster interaction between incoming and domestic students. There has also been support for some schemes seeking to promote curricular innovation, particularly those that aim to strengthen the European dimension within courses and degrees.

WORK PLACEMENTS

While regular student academic exchanges are the basis of Socrates/Erasmus activities, the Programme also offers other ways of studying abroad. One such is the work placement. Until recently, work placements did not feature prominently in UK exchanges but future EU plans envisage a considerable development of projects in this area. To be part of a Socrates/Erasmus exchange, the work placement has to contribute to a larger study framework and to be approved as part of it. A minimum of three months of academic coursework is required to provide a real disciplinary content. The ones that are currently offered generally involve paid work and are favoured particularly by students looking for vocational experience and hoping for financial returns. There is also a separate programme, Leonardo da Vinci, outside the exchanges, which is devoted primarily to providing opportunities in vocational training, and some institutions use this, too, to arrange placements for their students.

Setting up work placements generally involves the institutions which offer them in a great deal of effort, and they are expensive to operate because individual supervision arrangements may be required. They are also more relevant for some subjects than others. This, perhaps, explains why they have not been widely prevalent in UK exchanges. Indeed, outside particular areas, such as applied science, languages or business studies, they have often been quite hard to find. Even when they are available, not all provide lucrative employment. Sometimes, the financial gain is dubious which seems to limit their viability, at least in some participants' eyes. None the less, there is evidence that many students prefer to combine study with work (before, during and after term) when this is available and, with stronger backing from the Commission, demand for work-placement projects is widely expected to grow.

INTENSIVE COURSES

As well as regular term-time university courses, Socrates/Erasmus provides support for some intensive-study programmes. These are generally short courses, of ten days to three weeks in duration, commonly held during university vacations. They bring together in one location, often with outside experts, teaching staff and students from several universities and several different EU countries. They work particularly well in areas such as geography or language study where the local environment contributes directly to the interest.

Some commentators argue that the brevity of intensive courses tells severely against them, as they scarcely offer more than a taste of what is to be gained from intercultural studies. But there is evidence that the taste often proves appetising, and the participants are induced to go abroad on their own subsequently to deepen their cultural understanding. Intensive courses are more manageable for students with family or work ties at home, many of whom find year-long study difficult. But such courses are again in limited supply and are not available in many academic fields.

FINANCIAL SUPPORT

One of the main attractions of the Erasmus/Socrates programme is the financial support it offers. You are commonly given some assistance with such matters as the cost of travel, living costs and language-learning costs, where the language to be learned is one less widely used and studied. This is supplementary to any public grants or loans for which you are eligible at home. In other cases, the host EU country will offer support, sometimes by providing discounted language courses, sometimes by helping with accommodation costs or in a variety of other ways. And, as with most exchanges, the regulations of the programme specify that no student can be charged tuition fees by the host institution, nor any of a list of other academic charges (registration, examination) which might otherwise be payable.

There are, however, some important qualifications and exceptions. Each member state is provided with an overall financial allocation for student support which it then, in turn, allocates to individual institutions and they to the student participants, as is judged appropriate. As a result, the amount available for individual students does vary. It varies also, of course, in terms of the choice of host country, because the cost of living and travel is rightly held to be very different for different countries. More crucially, EU financial aid is provided primarily to benefit its own citizens. Those UK students who are not citizens of the European Union find that, while they are usually entitled to apply for a place, they are not entitled to share in all aspects of financial support. If they are offered a place, they normally won't have to pay fees to the host institution but they will still be liable for fees at home. They will also be ineligible for Erasmus grants for living costs. If you are not an EU citizen, care needs to be taken, therefore, to ensure that any general information issued on these programmes does apply to everyone.

THE CHARTER

A code of practice governing studying and teaching is found in most UK institutions. Internationally, such statements are much more unusual. The European Union has gone some way to rectifying this. It tries to provide some minimum service guarantees in the form of its Erasmus University Charter and Erasmus Student Charter. Neither document is meant to be entirely prescriptive or restrictive. Few students would turn first to the Charter when registering a complaint. None the less, the documents do indicate that all universities which participate in Erasmus/Socrates have agreed to the general rules governing the programme and have been recognised as being able to provide the standards which are judged appropriate.

The main benefit for you is to have a clear statement in advance about the terms of the programme and your right to have the studies recognised. It may also help to have it specified that any state financial assistance will be continued, where that applies. In return, there are a few obligations to which you are expected to conform. These include commonsense provisions on respecting the rules of the programme and of the host institution, keeping the home and host university in agreement with any changes made to study plans, and remaining in residence until the end of the agreed study period. There is also a more curious, though quite sensible, requirement that students must write a report on their study period abroad after they return. As the Charter is enforceable primarily through each university's own appeal procedures, however, it hardly constitutes a fundamental right. But it can be consoling to those with concerns.

OTHER EUROPEAN UNION PROGRAMMES

In addition to Socrates/Erasmus, which operates only within Europe, the European Union has adopted a number of programmes which allow for students moving to and from the wider world. The first of these was TEMPUS, a programme aimed initially at the countries of East and Central Europe, some of which have since become full members of the Union. Today the eligible countries are Albania, Bosnia and Herzegovina, Croatia, Macedonia, Yugoslavia, Armenia, Azerbaijan, Belarus, Georgia, Kazakhstan, Kyrgyzstan, Moldova, Tajikistan, the Russian Federation, Turkmenistan, Ukraine, Uzbekistan and Mongolia. In some respects, the TEMPUS programme, which is jointly funded and directed by the European Union and its partners, is seen as a contribution to development in these states as much as an educational initiative. It concentrates on the perceived priorities of the states themselves, generally involving infrastructural needs, rather than trying to ensure that student mobility is always included. Small numbers of students, however, do move in both directions within TEMPUS, and there are plans to increase this element significantly in future.

There are also programmes which operate with the United States, Canada, Latin America, China, South Asia, Australia and New Zealand, Africa, the Pacific and Caribbean. All of these have an individual focus, often on postgraduates, but the intention generally is to improve relations between the governments involved and broadly to assist in promoting mutual understanding through educational projects and student-centred activity. This usually means providing support for programmes of educational co-operation and programmes which tend to harmonise educational systems. The programmes chosen are all highly selective, both in terms of subjects and eligible students, so that most individual universities are little involved. None the less, as with TEMPUS, you should be aware of these programmes as possible sources of further Study Abroad opportunities.

POSTGRADUATE PROGRAMMES

Postgraduate students played only a very small part in the early days of the European programmes. Subsequently, more places were allocated to them and, today, interested postgraduates should certainly enquire. Even some research students, who initially were judged ineligible, have been successfully incorporated. Two of the current EU programmes, Jean Monnet, which deals with research in EU integration, and the Sixth Framework, in support of research promotion, are open only to research students. Recently, taught-course postgraduates have also been targeted directly, with the introduction of a programme for Masters degree students, Erasmus Mundus.

This is a degree programme which includes a Study Abroad element. It is highly selective and is currently available only in a small group of universities and only in narrowly defined fields. Erasmus Mundus takes the form of courses offered jointly by three or more institutions in three or more EU states, and you are required to do part of your studies in at least two. Awards are made jointly by the universities that you attend.

This scheme is quite different from Socrates/Erasmus. It is meant to be a showcase for European educational excellence in the wider world, and one major aim is to attract students from outside Europe. It is also extremely well funded, with generous scholarships for the incoming non-EU participants. For the European candidates, it is envisaged that some will do part of their study at institutions outside Europe and, for this, scholarships (less generously) are again made available. Every programme offering the option of allowing students to study outside Europe has to make arrangements to provide suitable places for them by including non-EU universities within its consortium. All of this indicates something of interest principally to the gifted few. Erasmus Mundus is best seen as a counterpart to the hugely prestigious American Fulbright programme which, for years, has distributed funds to enable distinguished young scholars to move between the rest of the world and the United States.

OTHER UK PROGRAMMES IN EUROPE AND BEYOND

In addition to EU programmes, British students have long been offered opportunities to undertake work and study elsewhere through exchange schemes administered by the British Council. One of the oldest and best known is called IAESTE. It is a summer programme, aimed chiefly at scientists, and offers them an opportunity to do some work/study with scientists elsewhere in the world. Science students have always found it easier to find work placements within a laboratory or research facility than non-scientists. But that is not to say that such places are in plentiful supply. The evidence suggests that they have been getting harder to obtain over the years, even though remaining popular, as the lines between work and study have become more tightly drawn.

The corresponding scheme in the humanities is probably the Year in Europe programme which is intended for language students with an interest in teaching. It offers an opportunity to work as a language assistant in an area where language skills can be honed and polished. Again, this depends on the co-operation of others to provide the placements. There has been a decline in numbers over the past few years, mainly, it appears, because the numbers training to become language teachers in the United Kingdom have also declined. In addition to programmes aimed at students, there are others, both within and outside EU auspices, which are meant for 'youth' or 'young learners' and to which occasionally students have resort. Finally, a small number of individual universities have set up their own bilateral programmes with European partners, outside Erasmus/Socrates.

BOLOGNA

In 1999, at a meeting in Bologna, European Union ministers agreed to move beyond student exchange by trying to standardise further- and higher-education qualifications throughout the whole organisation. One aim was to ensure comparability between degrees and so enable students more easily to move between one national educational system and another. Subsequently, it was suggested that the standard model should consist of a bachelor degree, lasting in general three or four years and constituting the undergraduate portion (or 'first cycle') followed by a master degree, usually of one or two years (the 'second cycle'), and then a doctoral degree, usually of three years (predictably, the 'third cycle') to complete the postgraduate portion. The template may look familiar as it owes a good deal to practice in the United Kingdom. The intention is to create what is called, rather uninspiringly, a European Higher Education Area (don't even try the acronym) and to allow students to gain access to the job market with qualifications recognised as equivalent throughout the Union.

Bologna is thought to carry with it a challenge for the United Kingdom. British students have been less inclined to study abroad in the European Union than their counterparts elsewhere. Will they be less able to avail themselves of the freer European job market and more subject to competition for jobs at home? The same concern extends to education. If students from elsewhere in the European Union have more assured rights of access in choosing to study in Britain, will competition for places in popular institutions be likely to grow? Providing extra places for any surplus demand or displacing it elsewhere might be possible but not without involving a considerable commitment from individuals and from government in the United Kingdom. Or will UK students find the Bologna structures, once fully implemented (and they are already having an impact, even beyond the European Union), make the opportunities and benefits of studying abroad seem altogether clearer?

STUDENT SOCIETIES

One of the strengths of European programmes, particularly Erasmus/Socrates, has been the support offered by student organisations. Different groups are involved – AEGEE: the National Unions of Students in Europe; ESIB: the European Union of Students in Europe; and ESN: the Erasmus Students Network. All share a commitment to the future of the European Union and a desire to ensure that visiting students are well supported. Many of these organisations try to help you find accommodation. Many more are involved with social programmes designed to introduce you to the local culture and to familiarise you with the country in which you have come to live. In the United Kingdom, where welfare provision is strong, programmes aimed at all students are often favoured over those making sectional provision for only some, and European student societies tend to be relatively small and modest in their activities. But in continental countries, with a clearer field, they generally exhibit far more ambition and enthusiasm.

Almost all of these societies arrange for programmes of visits to places of interest within the host country. Many of them also arrange social get-togethers in halls or clubs or bars or restaurants. These occasions are often held regularly or frequently so that a sense of community develops among the overseas participants and friendships are formed. Primarily they are an attempt to evoke the unity which the European Union itself reflects, an opportunity to explore culture contact within a group which finds this notion relatively congenial, attractive and safe. Their drawback is that they seem to attract few local students, other than the organisers and the real enthusiasts, into their ranks.

BRITAIN AND THE EUROPEAN UNION

Britain has one of the more unusual patterns of participation within European educational programmes. Under Socrates/Erasmus it attracts inwards over twice as many students as it sends out. The imbalance among full-degree students studying abroad is larger still. Most observers attribute this in part to the language of instruction. English is the preferred second language in almost every member country where it is not in use as the first one, which makes for a regular supply of candidates with the necessary linguistic skills. English has undoubtedly become the dominant language of global communication. An education in English can provide a preparation for careers world-wide, which is obviously a major attraction. The quality of education in the United Kingdom is also widely understood and highly respected, further adding to the appeal.

But while its inward mobility is strong, the United Kingdom has found it rather harder to match these numbers by persuading its students to study in the rest of Europe. Language is again cited most frequently as the explanation. The decline of late in the numbers of pupils and students in Britain studying languages decreases the pool of likely candidates here. Several attempts have been made to make study elsewhere in the European Union more attractive for UK candidates, not least by the UK government. One such is the fee waiver which is offered.

UNITED KINGDOM FEE AND SUPPORT ISSUES

The UK government currently arranges to pay the fees of all students in England, Wales and Northern Ireland who go abroad for an academic year on a Socrates/Erasmus programme, if they are eligible for support and would normally themselves pay the 'home' fee for that period. Other Erasmus students (including nearly all Scottish students studying in Scotland), who normally have their fees paid for them by government, continue to do so while they are abroad. Those going abroad on a credited study placement, outside Erasmus, and who, in consequence, attend for no more than ten weeks in the year at home, are also currently given government encouragement. They are usually exempted from half of any fee charge for that year which they would normally pay themselves. These concessions, however, will be overtaken by new tuition arrangements announced for September 2006 and will have to be revisited and perhaps replaced at that point.

Fee waivers are not the only sign of UK government support. Efforts have also been made to increase publicity for EU programmes and to offer those who undertake them competitions with prizes. All of this has not been without effect. If the whole of the European Union is regarded as a single market, then the United Kingdom sends well over half its Study Abroad students there. But there is a further explanation for the imbalance – the appeal to British students of studying in English in another anglophone country. The United States has long been the United Kingdom's favourite destination for studying abroad, and Australia and New Zealand have recently been in growing demand. Bringing the European numbers into balance can seem a Sisyphean task.

SUMMARY

EU educational programmes:

- Grow and develop
- Include short courses and postgraduate courses
- Offer student organisational and financial support
- Set out codes of conduct
- Extend beyond Europe
- Are supplemented by other official programmes
- Produce UK exchange imbalances

SOME QUESTIONS

Which office in your institution handles European programmes? Are there different offices for the Erasmus/Socrates programme and others? How is the information about European programmes communicated to students? What are the deadlines you need to observe? What programmes are open to you automatically and which by negotiation? Why might you choose Europe over other possibilities?

7 THE UNITED STATES

'A Scottish accent is a massive social asset here.'

'Make friends with people over twenty-one.'

The United States of America is by some measure the largest single market for British Study Abroad students, a dominance it has held for a great many years. This chapter explores why the United States is so popular, considers where students go and looks at some issues that emerge for those who choose to study there.

WHY THE UNITED STATES?

The appeal of the United States as a Study Abroad destination for UK students is quite evident. It is by far the largest higher-educational system in the world and certainly one of the most prestigious. The language of instruction is English and the educational structures derive ultimately from British models. Where differences have developed, they are generally easily understood by UK students. The US division between a private and a public sector, for example, is much less marked in higher education in the United Kingdom, but not entirely unknown either. The generosity of provision of educational resources in the United States – libraries, laboratories, facilities – is also widely known and admired here, as elsewhere.

Many non-academic elements add a great deal to the appeal. The United States is one of the richest countries in the world but not the most expensive in which to live. Though much depends on where you live and on the current exchange rate (important caveats), students generally consider the cost of living to be similar to that in Britain. The United States also has a lifestyle which is widely admired, and as widely deplored and often imitated. American culture is universally familiar in Britain as a consequence of the popularity of US films, television and music. For many British people, there is a sense of a shared history, even if usually differently interpreted. Some sense a shared culture, too, which derives from the common use of English and from common political and social traditions. If this now flows in distinctive and unequal streams, each still influences the other. Finally, for many students there is the attraction of being able to look for jobs, on and off campus, and the opportunity this provides to experience something of American life outside the classroom.

QUALITY

The primary attraction of the United States is, of course, that many of its individual institutions are considered to be among the very best in the world (though not everyone can hope to find places there). A few have long-established connections with universities in Britain. Sometimes there are 'twinning arrangements' which means that the partners are generally well known and highly regarded. Like Europe, the United States can boast centres of excellence in virtually every field of study that UK students favour. In total, it offers an unrivalled degree of choice, of institution, of course, of approach. And, though the American system is much more diverse than that of the United Kingdom, the two are felt on the whole to fit together quite well. Students moving between them have almost always found this to be relatively smooth and harmonious, though seldom effortless.

But, while the sheer size and diversity of educational provision in the United States are impressive – there are said to be over 4,000 post-secondary-education institutions – this presents you with difficult decisions. Institutions range in reputation from the world-class leaders, where nearly everyone would want to study, to places serving a local community and without any serious pretensions to sophistication or prestige, which you might prefer to avoid. Fortunately, the problem is readily solved. Higher education in the United States is probably more written about, dissected, analysed and classified than any other area of education in the world. It is quite easy to find league tables to categorise almost any kind of institution. Often, lengthy descriptions are available of the status, past and current, of individual colleges and universities. These may not immediately relate to the needs and interests of a British student but they will go a long way towards meeting those, too.

GETTING HELP

Given the size and diversity of provision, it is fortunate that most British Study Abroad students are presented with a selection of institutions by their home university rather than having to begin the search for themselves. But, if you have to make a choice, it tends to be easier to manage in the United States. The main source is the Bureau of Educational and Cultural Affairs of the US State Department. It publishes various guides and maintains a helpful website. There are also several well-known professional associations, each with its own website and set of publications, to guide you. The biggest and best known are the Institute of International Education, NAFSA (the national association of international educators) and the Council on International Educational Exchange.

All these have a primary interest in outgoing as well as incoming students, so you may have to search out the information they offer from among accounts meant for those moving in the opposite direction, from rather than to the United States. None the less, within both categories, they offer a comprehensive coverage. Their advice ranges from what to consider on first deciding to study abroad, through trying to find funding and making a selection of places, up to finally completing study and receiving transcripts. The range of studies covered is also very wide. It includes work placements and EFL programmes as well as undergraduate and postgraduate degree courses. One minor problem is that the term Study Abroad is often used in the United States to apply to full-degree as well as to occasional study. Once this is understood, anyone using these agencies to research study opportunities will generally be well rewarded.

RANKINGS

If you are hoping to make your choice by assessing the reputations of American institutions, you again have the backing of the US government in your search. Often, institutions are required by law to gather and publish information to aid enquirers – though you should remember that this makes them particularly skilled at self-presentation. Anyone who turns to the educational edition of *US News* (which is largely academic in focus) or to *The Princeton Review* (which includes social life – dormitories, food, fraternities) will immediately realise the help this provides. There you can search for a detailed directory of every institution, its history, current offerings, its wealth, its graduate placements, its safety record and dozens of other matters. You can also find information to allow you to judge between institutions, since there are almost endless comparative tables. These are usually available broken down by type of institution, geographical area and level of study. There are often articles, too, with information about whatever topics are currently in debate in the US higher-education sector.

The methodology employed in such rankings is always explained but this often makes for tedious reading and it may not be entirely clear to a reader from outside the United States. Its full relevance to the needs of an overseas student is also uncertain. It is wise, therefore, in making your decision, to be a little sceptical about place order within rankings, particularly where this relates to marginal differences. What you need is a general sense of where the institutions that interest you stand in relation to the group as a whole. Other factors matter, too, such as the size of the institution, its major subjects of study, its private or public status, and its classification (national university, liberal arts college, comprehensive college, specialist school), and all these are usually easy to establish objectively.

THE OPTIONS

The United States of America is a vast country. How do you decide where to study? As with many other countries, those looking for exchange places tend to concentrate their search on two or three main regions, while other areas are much less in demand. One of the most popular is undoubtedly the north-east, particularly New England. This is where the bulk of the highly regarded institutions of the 'Ivy League' are to be found (just like the plant which gives them their name). It is also a region with some major state universities, celebrated technical schools, impressive liberal arts colleges, and high-ranking institutions in every category of study. Academic type rather than geography seems to determine the label. Institutions regarded as typical of the north-east are found in other states of the eastern seaboard, ranging well beyond New England, into Maine to the north and certainly as far south as Pennsylvania, with outposts even further south still.

The second main group in demand in Britain is found in California in the far west. Again an area with a dense concentration of institutions, it includes some with reputations which match the best of their eastern rivals. California tends perhaps to have more provision in the public sector than does the north-east but offers a similar degree of diversity. In general, the student body there is drawn less from outside the immediate region, though that does nothing to diminish its appeal. Localism is usually positively attractive to students from abroad. A third main group is that of the mid-west, often envisaged as the institutions clustering round or to the south of the Great Lakes. This region, too, contains a number of universities and colleges which always feature among those in the top rank in any league tables, though less markedly so perhaps than with the other two.

The big three

For UK students, the distinctiveness of the north-east group probably lies in its prestige, in the fact that the institutions there are well known in Britain, and in its accessibility, being held to be the closest to Britain not only geographically but also culturally and socially. That is not to deny, of course, that it is also the birthplace of the Yankee, from whom European stereotypes of all that is distinctive about Americans derive. It is to the north-east that British Study Abroad students traditionally resort, and from the north-east that the bulk of US Study Abroad students in the United Kingdom come. The ease of communications between the two is no doubt one of its attractions. It is also an area which experiences four marked seasons (rather more markedly, in fact, than the British Isles usually), another element of familiarity.

The appeal of California relates partly to its prestige, partly to its 'West Coast' lifestyle (much envied and much mocked) and partly to the fact that it is seen as the most dynamic area in the United States today, having overtaken the north-east in this respect over the last half century. As with the north-east, its climate attracts but, in this case, largely because of differences. The absence of a sharp winter season – though the south and north of the state display important differences in this respect – is known to appeal to the sybaritic. Against the charms of the north-east and California, the mid-west appeals largely as the most authentically 'American' of the three principal regions, something that has always greatly interested British travellers. Those attracted by Americana find that the north-east and California are suspiciously cosmopolitan. The climatic appeal of the mid-west is also more exotic. The fascination of harsh winters and blazing summers is what students hope to find there.

Other regions

To select three regions is to ignore much of the wealth on offer. The general standard of higher education in the United States is famously reliable wherever you roam. The size of the country is often bewildering for British students. The fact that it has four time zones and that a journey across the continent by road can take well over a week seems devastating to anyone used to the much more manageable distances of Western Europe. But since air transport is plentiful and relatively cheap, these vast distances have been humbled, and there is no reason why those offered the possibility of studying outside the three main regions should feel concerned.

Education is principally a responsibility of each state in the United States, rather than of the national or federal government. Each state makes its own provision and all allow private competitors. The choice of institution is therefore everywhere generous, and quality, though it should still be checked, is not hard to find wherever you go. Some of the universities and colleges outside the Big Three, for example those in Texas, are virtually as well known and highly regarded as any. Across all the states, there are individual institutions where British students have been accommodated successfully.

NUMBERS

You should not push the notion of a special educational relationship between Britain and United States too far. There is no doubt that British students are not alone in finding the United States an attractive educational destination. Taking international students at all levels and using the latest figures, the leading sending nations are India, China, Korea, Japan, Taiwan and Canada. Even among European countries, the United Kingdom is second to Germany in absolute numbers and not far ahead of France. There is a marked volatility about international student numbers in the United States, and particularly about rank order. But it is clear that many, if not most, of the students from the leading countries are studying for full degrees. In Study Abroad, most observers would suggest, the United Kingdom, which once totally dominated, still has a leading position.

Despite their numbers, British Study Abroad students say that they seldom feel ghettoised or cut off from local students in the United States, as they can do elsewhere. One reason may be that international students are spread widely across the institutions and fields of study. Only around thirty universities and colleges boast more than 3,000 international students and only about 150 have more than 1,000. An emphasis on integration in a traditionally immigrant society may also be a factor. On the other hand, many find that Americans themselves are more ethnically diverse and culturally complex than their popular television image had suggested.

STUDIES IN THE UNITED STATES OF AMERICA

The standard American undergraduate degree lasts four years and is basically structured on a two-year general and two-year specialist basis. Almost all American institutions require students to take a variety of subjects (usually from a number of different disciplinary groups) in their early years, whatever their principal interests, and to specialise subsequently to some extent. This makes it relatively easy for Study Abroad students to find courses of the nature and level they require. But there are differences, too. In many 'liberal arts' places, at least, the requirements will include not only academic subjects but other contributions to student life, such as sports participation and social commitments, though these are not likely to be obligatory for visiting students.

Most institutions do offer 'majors', a near equivalent of 'honours' in the United Kingdom, generally a subject or subjects chosen as a specialist field for the final years of study. There are often single majors and double majors, rather like single and double honours. But there is unlikely to be a detailed honours curriculum, such as is common in Britain. Courses tend to be more self-contained, rather than sequential in the UK tradition. 'Majors' are often combined with 'minors', subjects in which the student does some element of specialisation but to a lesser extent than for majors, again something less commonly found in honours courses in Britain. Eligibility for courses also has its differences. Courses do tend to be graded by level of difficulty or sophistication, as in the United Kingdom, but this can extend in the United States up to those taken by master's students, and all levels are generally open to suitably qualified and ambitious candidates.

ASSESSMENT

The work which students are expected to perform is often regarded as the element which most clearly distinguishes American practice from practice in the United Kingdom. Almost all UK students find the work demanded heavy. You have to get used to an unremitting round of papers and essays and projects which each course seems to expect. It can be startling to find that there are often required reading hours and set reading. Gradually it dawns that these differences are explained by different and what is often seen as more egalitarian educational goals. This realisation then usually produces a reaction, a sense that the work demands are not simply different or more intensive but less intellectually demanding and less inclined to encourage independent thought. The reaction can persist. More often it changes eventually into a more balanced appreciation of the benefits of more directed work.

The marking system can also cause concern. A Grade Point Average (GPA) is used to record academic progress. It is a cumulative mark total, corresponding roughly to the average mark in all assessed work over all the courses taken. The GPA is a point of reference for lecturers giving access to their courses, employers filling jobs and students establishing pecking orders. It is an object of some concern for most US students to ensure that their GPA is annually maintained or improved, and this concern with grading can appear obsessive to outsiders. In Britain, where you are generally given marks for individual pieces of assessed work, these can be used to provide an indication of overall quality of performance. But class assessment is generally much lighter and in any case usually means a good deal less than performance in 'finals'. As a result, the US system, where every mark counts, can appear much more competitive. Yet, ironically, when the grades awarded to UK students under the system are higher than expected, this often seems to induce only an even greater scepticism about its merits.

PROFESSIONAL STUDIES

One of the clearest differences between US and UK practices lies in the way professional studies are taught. In the United Kingdom, subjects such as medicine and law are always available as undergraduate degrees (though, technically, entry into the profession usually requires an additional training qualification). In the United States, medicine and law are invariably postgraduate (or, as Americans would say, graduate) degree studies. Much of the basic disciplinary work in the United States does have to be completed as part of the bachelor degree and this makes the professional degree shorter than here. But all of the vocational study still has to be done after graduation. As a result, British students in these disciplines seeking study abroad in the United States usually have to be allowed a special dispensation to take graduate courses while still undergraduates (though, as already noted, this is, in terms of the grading of courses, by no means a unique exception).

Occasionally, differences also appear in mainstream science and mathematical subjects and languages. In Britain, the tradition is for such subjects, when taken at university, to build on a knowledge gained at school. In the United States, the tradition is to introduce all such subjects largely from scratch. Given also the need for a spread of subjects in the early years, this tends to mean differences in the content of courses, too. The differences probably have more of an impact on US students studying in Britain than on British students studying in the United States, but they are often real and occasionally result in misunderstanding. When choosing courses in this area, it is always wise to check not only the level but the prerequirements and the detailed content, too. Fortunately, most US institutions (unlike many in the United Kingdom) can provide that information in advance quite readily.

SOCIAL LIFE

The social life of American educational institutions almost invariably attracts great plaudits from British students. American students are seen as friendly, outgoing and optimistic. There are usually numerous opportunities for social interaction, particularly within dining halls and dormitories, where the tradition of sharing rooms (not always welcomed by British students and often avoided) is much more entrenched than in Britain. Some features of social life do raise eyebrows – the Masonic nature of fraternities and sororities, especially, though they have their supporters, too. But, generally, there are few complaints and many commendations.

Sadly, one feature of American student life has proved harder to swallow. The law does not permit the sale of alcohol to those below the age of twenty-one. Furthermore, this is enforced with rigour and righteousness. Most British Study Abroad students seem to feel the element of age discrimination keenly, even when not unsympathetic to the policy in general. But there is no doubt that the benefits of an alcohol-free lifestyle are not always fully grasped by those most concerned. As in the 1920s, when the feeling was more universal throughout society, complaints about prohibitionism are rife. Fortunately, the pecuniary gain is sometimes held to outweigh the need for personal sacrifice.

HEALTH AND SAFETY

For the United States, you will have to obtain health insurance because health care there is entirely private. This adds a little to the usual living costs but is not something that under any circumstances should be ignored. There are extra risks in being abroad, simply from unfamiliarity, and everyone needs to be properly insured in order to feel secure. A very wide choice of policies is available and everyone has to decide what particular risks might be worth considering. Dangerous sports or unusual hobbies, such as bungee-jumping or cyclone watching, for example, may necessitate some serious extra cover, and that can be expensive.

The other significant concern among British students seems to be over security. High crime rates in particular districts and the availability of guns in the United States have long attracted the attention of the British press and no doubt the publicity greatly exaggerates the danger. None the less, some American institutions, concerned by the reputation, take active steps to provide you with extra protection – escorting students to and from late-night events, for example. Others argue, with strong evidence to support them, that they have no need to be particularly concerned. In the last resort, personal security has to be left to your own common sense. It is often enough simply to be aware of it and to avoid situations that might prove problematic.

SUMMARY

The United States appeals to UK students on grounds of:

- Quality of institutions
- Advice available
- Variety and choice
- Distinctiveness and compatibility
- Ease of integration

Differences can arise with:

- Professional subjects
- Attitudes to assessment
- The need for insurance
- Personal security issues

SOME QUESTIONS

What would persuade you to choose the United States over other study destinations and what would make you hesitate to do so? How would you propose to meet the costs of studying in the United States? What choice of studies in the United States does your institution offer?

8 GETTING ADVICE AND APPLYING

'Read the information from the home and host universities so that you know what you are supposed to be doing. It makes life much easier.'

'I missed the chance to talk to former exchange students before I left. That was a mistake.'

Everyone would agree that studying abroad, even when no problems arise, can be quite demanding. It is not the easy option, the 'holiday from studies', which it is sometimes presented as being. It offers you a lot but requires a lot from you. If you are to take it on, you have to be confident that you can cope. Above all, you have to search out and to be able to use good advice. This chapter deals with that and then with applying. Everyone contemplating Study Abroad needs to apply promptly. The arrangements which have to be made are extensive. Things can go wrong and you need to allow time to sort out any problems. If you are competing with others for a place, you also need to make your application as attractive and forceful as possible to catch the eye of the selectors.

BASICS

Before you decide to apply, it is very important that you should first be convinced that studying abroad really is worthwhile. You should know not only what you are taking on but also why. Of course, studying abroad may be one of your degree requirements. That leaves you with little option. But you should still give the matter some thought. Most observers believe that, if you can see the benefits, you have gone some way to realising them. If Study Abroad is not compulsory, the importance of deciding what you are to gain from it is even more crucial. You need to be sure that it suits you and that it adds to the interest in your degree. It helps also to know that this study has the backing of your university advisers, particularly of your school or department (not something which you should assume) and that you will get encouragement and support when you undertake it. Without that, you may be unwise to proceed.

If you are required or just encouraged to study abroad, you will probably be supplied with some printed information. Everyone finds that helpful. Often, advisory sessions will be arranged with the administrative staff responsible for the programme where you can discuss possibilities and clarify any points about which you are uncertain. Some universities collect questionnaires from all students returning from studying abroad and then file their responses for prospective exchange students to consult. If such documents are available, they often prove to be a mine of useful information as they are usually written when the experience is still recent and raw. It is worth spending some time on them. They can give a very clear view about how it feels to be a student abroad and what problems you might encounter.

PERSONAL ADVICE: STUDENTS

Usually, once you have expressed an interest, a briefing session is arranged with a number of students from your field of studies who have taken part in the programme in the previous sessions. If this is not routinely done, you can always set up an informal session yourself by inviting a few returnees for coffee and a chat. The Study Abroad office will put you in touch. This is an opportunity to hear a more considered and longer-term verdict than questionnaires provide. The advice can be particularly revealing when it comes directly from fellow students and when you can interrogate them. But, of course, you still have to evaluate what you are told. You need to make some allowances for any differences between their situation and yours. You are likely to find that some of them are hugely encouraging and enthusiastic, and there will also be a few, probably, who sound doubtful or dismissive. It is important to listen to, and to be critical of, both. You also have to sort out the bits that seems objective and universal from those that may relate to individual experiences.

Returned exchange students are particularly good at conveying their feelings. They will be proud of having done this study before you and keen that you should learn from their example. They won't mince words if they feel that anything was amiss, and they will tend to shoot from the hip. This is enormously helpful because you can then ask for reassurance from the university authorities on any awkward points they raise with you. The one danger is that you may get the impression that their experience is shared more widely than in fact it is. We all tend to assume that our experience is a universal one. One or two of them may even be playing to the gallery. As you are providing a captive audience, some overacting is to be expected. To get round the problem, you should try to speak to more than one person if you can.

PERSONAL ADVICE: ACADEMIC STAFF

It helps to talk matters over with a member of the academic staff in your own area of studies. Where exchanges are required, arrangements will probably be made for you to do this, possibly through an initial group meeting and then individual consultations. The advice given by academic staff has a different importance. Academics belong to quite a small world. They often have contacts in the partner institutions and they may have spent time there or know something of its reputation, its strengths and weaknesses. Their advice is particularly helpful about how your subject is taught there and about any differences between that and study at home. They will also probably know how the courses abroad fit into the studies at home. If you want to choose courses which complement your studies at home, they are going to be particularly helpful. Even if you want to escape as far as possible from your current studies and try something new, they should be in a good position to advise.

Academic staff are also the guardians of the history of an exchange. They will know how students have fared in the past and what kind of reputation the exchange has gained. They will be able to say, for example, if credit transfer ever proved a problem. They may have views on whether students encounter difficulties with some subjects or courses or seem to get an enormous amount out of others. They will be able to assess if students on the exchange improved their academic performance thereafter or encountered unexpected obstacles and difficulties on their return. From observations like these, you can begin to get a picture of what you are taking on and to sense how much of a leap is involved. Quite often, this is very encouraging, as most staff seem to believe that studying abroad can be truly beneficial.

BASIC ACADEMIC REQUIREMENTS

In applying for Study Abroad, you will be expected to demonstrate your suitability. The first thing you will need is a sound academic record. Study Abroad programmes are almost never available to students in their first year, so your record at university is commonly used to determine whether or not you can go. In some cases, you will be expected not only to do well generally but also to have an especially good record in a particular subject. The assumption is not that the overseas courses will be particularly difficult. It is simply that you will face different demands from being abroad. Ensuring that you are a competent student is a kind of safeguard against any problems that may arise.

When you have had difficulties with your university studies at home, it may be unwise to contemplate studying abroad altogether. Study Abroad is best not regarded – as sometimes it seems to be – as an ordeal which you must undergo in order to redeem your past. But you certainly need not be the top student in your class to apply. Studying abroad means joining in with local students who will be as varied in ability as students at home. Because the studies and the work requirements are likely to be different in some respects, it is actually possible that these will suit you better and that you will improve on your performance at home. Many students do. But, even if you don't, you should gain something extra from the different experience and so still make progress academically and personally.

NON-ACADEMIC REQUIREMENTS

When studying abroad is voluntary and not a requirement for the whole class, and there are limits on the numbers permitted to go, a selection procedure is then used. This probably involves an application form and interview. It is often suggested that to be selected for studying abroad you require two qualities, a good academic record and a good personal profile. Character and personality, in other words, are usually given weight as well as academic ability. Sometimes you will be told you must have 'ambassadorial qualities', meaning the capacity to give a good account of yourself abroad so as to reflect credit on your institution. An ambassador is generally thought to possess tact, courtesy, diplomacy, charm, social sensitivity and an understanding of people. That is what the selectors will be looking for in you. It may seem a tall order but you probably will get a long way, too, with just enthusiasm (if it is genuine) and pleasantness (if it is unfeigned).

The selectors will also be interested in your membership of societies, your hobbies, sporting activities, musical talents and other interests beyond the classroom. Those whose interests extend beyond their immediate studies are thought to cope better with the cultural demands of studying abroad. If you have wider interests, you are probably better able to see your studies in perspective and less concerned about taking on new challenges. You are also likely to involve yourself more in the different aspects of life abroad and so to get more from the experience. In making your application, it is wise to give some thought to how you might best present yourself so as to meet these various expectations.

Language skills

If you have to study in a language other than English, you will obviously need the requisite language skills. Normally, non-anglophone universities specify the tests they regard as acceptable evidence of your competence in the local language, and you obviously have to meet those. In general, the standard they expect is roughly equivalent to an A-level grade or a Higher grade in Scotland. Some accept many different kinds of proofs of competence; some need specific ones, such as stated levels of achievement in speaking, writing and listening in a named test. It is important to note, however, that any figure quoted for a test result is likely to be the minimum required. Those who supply the figure are assuming that, starting from this point, you will continue to improve. This is a reasonable assumption, after all, given that you are going to be living and working in an environment where you will be using the language daily.

If, for any reason, the assumption proves to be incorrect, the minimum requirement is unlikely to be sufficient. Very few of us have sufficient linguistic skills to regard ourselves as entirely at ease in another language. And even those who can make that claim sometimes face problems with local usage, dialect and slang. In any case, a minimally acceptable grasp of a language will not allow you to do your best work. You may have some difficulty understanding lectures and expressing yourself in essays or written work. Your social interaction with your fellow students may be impaired. Worse still, your excuses for late essays will become transparent and your chat-up lines will sound calculating. If your language level is only the minimum required, it is important that you should make every effort to improve before and during your studies abroad. Where your university offers term-time language courses for students studying abroad, it makes sense to take one. It will serve to refresh your memory, get your ear attuned to the different tongue and, hopefully, awaken or reawaken your enthusiasm for communicating across cultures.

METHODS OF APPLYING

The methods of applying for Study Abroad are as various as the programmes. If the time spent abroad is a requirement of your course and arrangements have been made to provide everyone with a place, you are likely to receive your application form from your own department or school. If not, you must obtain it yourself, which is generally not difficult to do. Once completed, the form will often be checked internally before being forwarded (in a batch, perhaps) to the university abroad. Even if you apply as part of a group, however, you are still personally responsible for the application made. When you are asked to enclose documentation, reference letters, a certificate of your academic record, essays, you must arrange for this to be done. The application may be used more widely than simply by the admissions office of your host institution. It may contain details requested by, and released to, immigration authorities, for example. A cavalier approach to completing the form is not recommended.

Those participating in non-required programmes may have to apply initially through their department or school and then face the selection process. Once the selection has been made and places allocated, the applications forms will be sent to you. Candidates successful at interview are usually asked to complete the form and submit it by a specified date. Again, it is possible that your application will be checked by someone in your own institution before it is sent off. Again, you should not see this as a reason to treat the matter lightly. Study Abroad programmes can involve many different institutions and a whole variety of different application forms. It is up to you to be certain that you have followed the directions required by your particular host institution. You can, of course, always ask for assistance from your own university if necessary.

Application formalities

Sometimes the application form will not be in English and, even if it is, it is likely to be unfamiliar to you in different ways. For example, you are sometimes asked about matters which would not normally appear on a British form, such as your blood type or your medical record. Laws on confidentiality or data protection don't always operate internationally (particularly not outside the European Union). The terms used in the form may be unfamiliar to you or may be used in a way which makes them sound unfamiliar. Your exposure to another culture has begun! The only sensible approach is to treat all this as a learning exercise and to seek help from your advisers if any of the questions involve issues about which you are uncertain or which make you feel uncomfortable.

You may also have to gather together some information in order to respond. Apart from producing language certificates, you may be asked to write an essay about your host country or your host institution or to enclose a specimen of your academic work. If this has to be in a language other than English, the intention may be to see how fluent you are. It might help to get your efforts checked over by a native speaker, though it is not altogether a good idea to give an impression of fluency which, in fact, you don't possess. If you have to write in English, the essay may be used to discover how motivated you are in your studies and what interest you have in benefiting from your time abroad. The information is not likely to be used to exclude you. Rather it may be designed to be of use to those who will be required to advise you within the host institution and whose job is to find a programme there which is going to suit you best.

Transcripts

Nearly all application forms will ask you for a transcript. A transcript is simply an account of your academic studies in university or college up to the present. It details all the courses you have taken and the grades or marks you have obtained in each course. Inevitably, because you are likely to have to apply while you are in the middle of one session in order to study in the next, the transcript will list some courses for which you do not yet have final grades or marks. A decision on admission will usually be made on the basis of what you have already achieved, perhaps subject to your successfully completing the outstanding courses.

A transcript is an official document and it often bears an institutional stamp and is signed by someone in authority in your university. You normally obtain it from the central Registry. There may be a charge for issuing it which you may have to pay. Perhaps in an effort to save you that expense, some universities abroad are willing to accept something slightly less formal than a transcript, provided it contains the same information, such as a signed letter on official paper from one of your academic advisers. But to guard against false claims and forgeries (security is a major concern in universities at present), even that may require an official stamp. Your academic adviser will know the practice that normally prevails at your institution and will guide you.

References

Almost all applications for Study Abroad require references. Usually, these must come from your academic tutors and advisers. You will have to decide which among them would be most enthusiastic about you and then approach them privately to ask if they are willing to oblige. It is sometimes easier when convention dictates whom you must prefer. If your referees are unsure about what to include, you can suggest that they write something about your academic ability and about your general character, and they might also make some mention of their impression of how well you are likely to cope with studies abroad. Choosing referees who have some knowledge of the country or institution to which you are going can be helpful but it is not vital. What you need is someone who will be positive about the prospects for you of studying abroad. References become particularly important when they are used in the selection process at home or in placing you in courses when abroad.

Technically, even when you are on a reciprocal exchange programme, the host university has the right to question or reject any applications. The references are therefore a guarantee that you have the support of your university and the good opinion of some of your tutors. It is, in fact, very rare for host universities to turn down applications once they have been vetted and approved at home. But these are not purely formal documents. The host university will want to know for its own security that you are of good character, that you are a serious-minded student and that you have the potential to do well in an international environment. To ask for confirmation of this in the form of references is only common sense, even if they take the more hyperbolic passages on your outstanding qualities (which will doubtless appear in them) with a grain of salt.

Passport formalities

Some applications ask you to send a photocopy of parts of your passport – in which case you will need to be sure that you have a passport and that it is up to date. At busy times of the year, a passport can take a few weeks to obtain. In some countries your passport has to be machine readable, and you may have to check that and replace your current one, if necessary. Sometimes you are told that your passport must be valid for up to a year after your arrival, and this, too, may necessitate a replacement.

If you do not hold a British passport, you should ask your own embassy or consulate to advise. There may be different instructions for you from those which apply to British passport holders, particularly if you come from outside the European Union. You will be subject to the rules that operate for your passport country. That may mean more complications or conceivably fewer. But it is something which you will probably have to investigate yourself rather than relying on the general instructions from your institution.

SUMMARY

Getting advice depends on exploiting contacts with:

- Student returnees/visitors
- Study Abroad offices
- Tutors and academic advisers

To succeed as an applicant, you may require:

- A sound academic record
- Ambassadorial qualities
- Appropriate language skills
- Timely application
- A transcript
- Supportive referees
- A valid passport

SOME QUESTIONS

Which offices in your university provide advice for those wishing to Study Abroad? Do you have to register your interest in order to be sent information or is this circulated to everyone? Where do you turn to if you need information which relates to studying abroad in your subject of study? When do you have to apply? What elements in your c.v. do you think will most appeal to selectors? If you want to study abroad, how useful would it be to prepare a timetable of all the things that need to be done?

9 MAKING PREPARATIONS TO GO: LONGER TERM

'I was surprised at the time it takes, and the expense, and how much information they need to issue you with a visa.'

'Save up before you come and look for a job on campus.'

The process of arranging to study abroad can be quite time consuming. You are often advised to begin making preparations a year or more before you are due to go. It can take anything up to three months at the beginning of the academic year to get the information you need to make a choice about country and institutions. Making a decision about exactly which courses to apply for can take up to another three months. If there is a selection process and interviews are arranged, this needs a month or so, too. Making your application and getting it checked can take another month. You may have to wait for a response from the overseas university, perhaps for one to three months. After that, you may have to obtain a visa, which could add yet another month. Of course, you may get by on far less time than that, particularly if most things are done for you, but you may not. This chapter offers an account of the preparations that need to be made and suggests how you might tackle them.

RESPONSIBILITY

How much responsibility for organising your time abroad is put on you depends partly on your university. If it supplies copious information and informed briefings, arranges for you to receive and to return the application forms, reminds you of crucial dates and then superintends your departure, your obligations will be fewer. If you have to obtain everything yourself, complete the forms correctly and observe all the deadlines, a certain amount (in some cases, an unusual amount) of organisation and discipline may be required. Obviously, self-respect will dictate that you should much prefer the latter, but you may be willing, generously, to tolerate the former.

The contribution of your host university is also uncertain. If it has a very highly developed system for dealing with visiting international students, you may from your first enquiry be supplied with helpful information, clear guides and constant encouragement. Unfortunately, it is also possible that you may be faced with forms which are difficult to follow, prospectuses which are fully intelligible only to the bureaucratic mind, and demands for information which seem as peremptory as police summonses. Asking you to be prepared well in advance is just a way of trying to ward off hassle, whatever situation you face.

STUDY PERMITS

Your first requirement is an official acceptance letter which should arrive in due course from the institution to which you have applied. Even before you have this and know that you have secured a place, you can begin making other preparations. If you are an EU citizen and intend to study within the European Union, you normally won't require a visa. But it is always worth checking because there are exceptions, and rules can change quite suddenly. For EU citizens going outside the European Union or non-EU citizens going elsewhere in the European Union, you will probably need a visa or at least a permit to reside as a student. You usually have to bring or send to the nearest embassy, consulate or high commission for the country you intend to visit some or all of the following: a completed application form, your passport, a copy of your letter of admission to your host university, extra passport photographs, proof of your financial standing such as a letter from a grant sponsor or a bank, and a letter from your own university certifying that you are a student and in good standing. You also sometimes require a particular form, often called a certificate of eligibility, which the host university obtains on your behalf from its immigration authorities and sends along with its letter of acceptance.

To find out exactly what you need and what you must present, you will have to get in touch with the immigration authorities yourself. The information is often available at the embassy address on the Internet. There can be a cost for getting the documents and it is not always small. Concerns about international terrorism and fears about illegal immigration have led many countries (including the United Kingdom) to be rather more cautious when issuing student residency permits. If you are put through the mill to obtain one, you may be willing to accept that any inconvenience caused is, in the last resort, the outcome of an attempt to ensure your safety.

VISAS

In most countries a student visa or residence permit differs from a visitor's visa. It generally allows you to stay longer, for example, and it gives you more rights, sometimes even including employment rights. Students with a visa or residence permit may still have to register with the city or town authorities on arrival (which most visitors do not) but are not then normally required to report again for their entire period of studies. Rules on such matters, however, often change and it is wise to check the latest position with the embassy or high commission or by looking up the information on the British Foreign Office website. A visa, incidentally, does not entirely substitute for a certificate of eligibility. If you have a certificate, it should always be kept inside your passport because it, too, may be required as proof of your immigration status.

If you need a visa, you are sometimes offered a choice between a single entry and multiple entry. When this occurs and you are quite certain that your visit to your host country will be unbroken, then the former will suffice. But many students use the opportunity of Study Abroad in one country to travel to neighbouring countries during the vacations, and they also sometimes return home for special events. It may be that a multiple-entry visa (though always more expensive) will be preferable. Sometimes in any case only multiple-entry visas are issued. Obtaining a visa involves some work as well as cost and often takes an unconscionable time to produce (it is not something that should be left until the last minute). But it does give you status as a temporary resident and you can check what rights it gives you to work or to leave and return.

Health issues

Some applications for an entry permit require you to provide evidence of your medical history. Even if this is not required or there is embarrassingly little for you to record, you need to give some thought to your health. The most obvious requirement is an insurance policy, covering likely eventualities for the period you are abroad. If you are an EU citizen and are moving within the European Union, your National Health Insurance should be sufficient to cover any medical treatment abroad. But you will need a form to prove your entitlement. This is usually obtainable from a post office or from a DHSS office in the United Kingdom. For almost all other categories of students and in all other countries, you will be expected to take out health insurance to pay for any treatment you might require. It may be worth checking first what protection is offered without insurance. In some countries the National Health Service in Britain has negotiated a reciprocal deal under which you are entitled to some medical protection. If none exists or if it seems insufficient for your purposes, an insurance policy will then be necessary.

Some universities overseas negotiate a health insurance package with a local company and then ask all its visiting students and probably all local students, too, to purchase it.

It could well be the best deal for you. You may even be required to obtain it as a condition of acceptance. That may seem an imposition but nobody wants to have to bail you out in an emergency when your insurance cover proves inadequate. If no such scheme operates, you can compare the costs of the different polices available in Britain and the coverage they provide, and then make your own choice. Dental needs should also be kept in mind. If you know you will require dental surgery, costs can mount up. It is certainly worth getting a dental check-up before you go.

MEDICAL PRECAUTIONS

You may need to take some preventive health measures before you leave. Even if the country you are going to has very high public health standards, it is still worth thinking about and checking your inoculations and vaccinations to ensure that these are appropriate and up to date. Obtaining these abroad may be too late (some preventive measures are effective only after several months of treatment) and can be expensive, whereas they are not generally so for students in the United Kingdom. Indeed, most students can get the bulk of the treatments free. Some universities abroad will insist on proof of immunity, such as evidence that you have been vaccinated against particular named diseases, something unusual in Britain except perhaps for medical students. You should be told if anything is needed, unless it is intended that the treatment will be provided after you arrive. Your doctor's surgery at home will give you a stamped vaccination certificate with an account of all the inoculations you have obtained from it, and you can keep this in your passport.

Taking medical precautions is not always a local stipulation, and it is true that in most countries and in most cities public health standards nowadays are high. There may, however, be various local issues of which you need to be aware. While a lot depends on where you are going and what you plan to do while there, travel, climate change and differences in diet can all affect your general health. Caution is always advisable, even though you may feel you are very unlikely to fall ill. A chat with a nurse or a doctor to decide whether anything needs to be done in advance is strongly recommended.

DISABILITY

The law on disability is not the same in every country. In Britain in recent years an effort has been made to ensure that disabled students are able to participate fully in higher education. This includes (or will include) such matters as gaining physical access to buildings and being allocated appropriate resources, such as enlarged texts, for those with visual disability, and special examination arrangements, for those with writing difficulties, for example. What prevails abroad is uncertain. You may find far better provision and discover that your host institution can cope with your every need. Or you may find that provision is so much inferior that it puts in doubt your interest in the programme.

It is too late to discover such problems only after you have arrived in your host institution. You need to give thought to what you require and to raise the matter with the host university when you think of applying. If you would prefer to do this discreetly and confidentially, your local Disability Office or Student Services office may be able to help. You must also be prepared for the fact that disability is often differently defined in other countries. There may be superb provision for the physically disabled, for example, but very poor provision for the dyslexic.

LANGUAGE PREPARATION

If you are going to a non-anglophone country, you may have decided to spend some time on improving your language skills in the months before you leave. This is not now a matter of meeting the entry requirements of your institution, which you will already know. It is much more because what you get out of the whole experience of being abroad is going to depend partly on how well you communicate, and that is very largely a matter of linguistic skills. Universities and language schools in Britain offer many different kinds of language-learning courses. Courses for special purposes often include the academic use of a language. Such courses also provide instructions on study skills. There is today a very flourishing market in language learning in Britain and elsewhere, and you will find that course fees vary in different institutions. The same can be true of the quality of instruction on offer. It may be best to ask what accreditation your language programme can boast before you commit yourself to it.

It is sometimes possible for you to spend the last part of the vacation period before you leave engaged on language learning, in which case it might be best undertaken abroad, costs permitting, and in the country in which you will study. Then, you can be certain that your instruction will expose you to the latest idioms and you may be able to get an insight into local teaching and learning styles, too, before you begin your course. In some cases, this kind of language-preparation course can be arranged through your host institution and its recommendation is usually a guarantee of quality. If you are arranging it on your own, it is again wise to check on what is available and at what cost. Courses with a strong emphasis on sightseeing trips and visits to the ballet are diverting but perhaps not always what you are looking for. It is also worth checking class size and class composition. Being in a large group of fellow citizens is often ideal for watching soccer matches but is seldom conducive to the best language learning.

READING AHEAD

With exchanges, you may be able to obtain reading lists for the courses you will take in advance. Particularly when you will be operating in a second language, it is useful to begin your study preparation as early as possible. Having mastered some of the required reading before you arrive, you will feel more confident about being able to take things in your stride. If you do encounter initial difficulties, the fact that you have already done some work gives you a bit more space and time. It may also indicate to you where your weaknesses in the subject lie and give you the opportunity to think of how to tackle them before you embark on the course.

You ought to choose the works that look most interesting to you and avoid those that look more complex or problematic. It doesn't help if you are already convinced that the course is difficult even before you have embarked on it. Reading without supervision and guidance is apt to maximise the obstacles, whereas reading once the lecturer has elucidated the subject can avoid that. There are usually a few texts on any reading list which look more familiar or seem more accessible than others and these pay better dividends as introductory reading. You should concentrate on those and leave the others till later.

FUNDING

In many cases, finding the funding to Study Abroad is not a problem. If you receive a student loan or a maintenance grant or bursary and are going on an official exchange, this is likely to be continued, though you do need to check and to inform the awarding body of your plans. A few aspects of extra support, such as travel payments, may not operate if you move abroad, unless this is a compulsory part of your course or for an Erasmus programme. On the other hand, Erasmus students and those who are required to Study Abroad may find themselves entitled to additional payments for travel or insurance as a result. This needs to be checked. You also need to arrange a contact address for funds to be forwarded and for next year's application forms to be sent to you. If costs are roughly the same abroad as at home and most of your current funding remains in place, the main issue to consider is the additional amount you sometimes need to find for international travel.

When you are not able to live as cheaply abroad as at home because of extra costs or because of your unfamiliarity with local circumstances, you will need to be able to make up that amount, unless assistance is routinely offered to those on the exchange. If there are no earmarked funds available, searching for other sources of funds is not going to be easy. In a very few cases, the programme will have its own scholarships, though these are often competitive. Most UK funds in support of higher education go to those engaged in postgraduate research. For undergraduates, it is likely that those doing a full degree abroad will be favoured over someone doing only occasional studies. Study Abroad is usually given the lowest priority of all. This makes it imperative that you have done your sums, worked out what your expenses are likely to be and decided how you are going to meet these, assuming no extra help is available.

Finding funding support

When there are grants or scholarships available attached to the programme and you are eligible, you will need no encouragement to apply. Otherwise, the main prospects of finding something probably lie with your local educational authority, your home university, your host university and private foundations. The information on all sources of financial assistance is often collected by your university and made available in the International or Study Abroad office, though this may simply be a statement that there is not likely to be any funding available for your programme. There may also be something on your university's website or on the website of your host university. Where funding is made available as part of the Study Abroad programme (as with Erasmus) the information will certainly be available in your university and will probably be communicated to you directly as part of the application process.

Apart from programmes with attached scholarships, most Study Abroad students who obtain funding do so through governmental sources. Local education authorities in the United Kingdom sometimes make awards to assist with travel or with the extra costs involved in living abroad even, very occasionally, when this is not part of Erasmus or a compulsory element in the course. It is certainly worth enquiring. There is always a limit to what can be allowed and special rules on what can be claimed. None the less, any extra help can often make a big difference. Looking for other bursaries in the United Kingdom or in your host country is possible but many feel that the results are not commensurate with the required effort.

Earning income

Depending on where you are going, you may be able to get a job abroad, which is another method of tackling any funding shortfalls. Some students, those visiting the United States and Japan, for example, by working part time in term time and full time in the vacations, sometimes claim to be able to earn more abroad than they do at home, and some say that they return better off than they left. This experience is certainly not universal. In some cases you will be prevented from taking employment because of your immigration status. You should find out when asking about visas. In others, you will be allowed to work but mainly in restricted and poorly paid jobs. In some, local unemployment will dictate that you will find it is virtually impossible to find a job. Before you leave, you ought to enquire into the prospects and into local rules on employment for students. Only if you are confident of having a job should you include a sum from earnings in your overall calculations.

The main problem with working your way through college is, of course, the time it takes. You cannot afford to take on a job that will distract you from your studies, because that is your primary purpose in being abroad. At most, you can probably afford to work only about a couple of hours a day, and there are not many jobs which conveniently fit these requirements. Working full time in vacations is much more viable, provided that you do not also have projects which you must complete during that time, and there may still be restrictions on the kind of work you can do. Where visas are required, there may also be time problems if you arrive in a country early or leave it late to take up work, as visas are time limited. You need to check. Some universities offer part-time jobs 'on campus'. These can sometimes be plentiful but they are seldom lucrative.

PROVIDED ACCOMMODATION

Finding a suitable place to stay concerns everyone. It is central to your sense of settling down well. Sometimes accommodation is arranged for you as part of your programme, which is obviously helpful, though problems can still arise. You are likely to have to apply without really knowing what your place will be like. You may even be given a choice but have little idea about what distinguishes one possible residence from another. If no informed advice is available to you locally, you may just have to trust to luck or to intuition. But at least you will then know where you will be staying, well in advance. That makes many things much easier. You can often send luggage on ahead. You can also inform your friends and your university of your address before you leave, which is a comfort to them. Since immigration officials sometimes expect you to provide a local address on arrival, you are in a position to respond to them, too.

Even so, you still have a few questions to consider. You will need to know when you will get access and how to obtain your key. The accommodation arrangements abroad may be different from those that you are familiar with at home. Will you be sharing or will you have a room of your own? Do you have to have bedding (sheets and pillowcases) or is this supplied? If you are to be cooking for yourself, do you have to provide crockery and cutlery and cooking implements or are these supplied? How do you get to your accommodation from the station or airport? How do you get from the accommodation to your university or college? How long does it take? Knowing the answers allows you to prepare more effectively and to pack what you might need.

PRIVATE ACCOMMODATION

If you have no place arranged and are expected to make your own arrangements, you will need to give thought to this. The vital thing is to have somewhere to stay at least for the first few days. There may be information about this in your home institution, perhaps provided in a guide for international students or in reports by students who went on the programme in earlier years. Today, the Internet is an enormously valuable resource on such matters. If you can find the e-mail address for the tourist information office in the country or city to which you are bound, you are usually in a position to find the accommodation available for short stays. Sometimes you can book on the Internet, so that everything can be arranged before you leave.

Looking to the longer term, you also need to exploit your local contacts. It is possible that your university will be able to suggest addresses where students have stayed before. It is worth searching on your host university's student website, as there is sometimes a page there for those trying to find flatmates. You must also get in touch with students from your own institution who were studying in the host one in the year before, as this may give you some leads. You may even be able to arrange to take over their accommodation or they may be able to provide good advice about where and how you should search. Personal contacts are often the best way to search out a good place. If all this fails, you may be able to find (or perhaps to place) advertisements for accommodation in the local press, in government offices or in housing agencies (the latter being, usually, the most expensive) as it is sometimes possible to do this from home.

SUMMARY

In making arrangements to go abroad, you need to give thought to:

- Your individual responsibilities
- Getting a study permit/visa
- Health requirements
- Language preparation
- Finding the funds
- Arranging accommodation

SOME QUESTIONS

What, if any, official documentation, such as a visa or residence permit, will you need to obtain before you can go abroad as a student? What advice on health precautions is available to you? How much help can you get from your own institution or your host institution in finding a place to stay?

10 MAKING PREPARATIONS TO GO: SHORTER TERM

'I found the process of coming over quite stressful and daunting.'

'Familiarise yourself a bit with the university and city before you leave and know what you have to do and where you have to go in the first couple of days.'

In the weeks before you leave, you need to think ahead to what will confront you on arrival. Being prepared for problems of adjustment, which many students report initially, can help you to cope with them. There is also the major question of packing to be faced and the need to come to terms with separation from home and attachment to something new abroad.

ARRANGING FOR THE TRANSFER OF FUNDS

You will certainly need some funds on first arrival and may have to make early payments for some quite major items, particularly if you are confronted immediately with such matters as paying fees or securing a let or furnishing an apartment. A credit card is probably best for large items but you will also need to take some local currency with you for smaller things. Local currency is now generally available in the United Kingdom for most of the countries to which you are likely to resort. You may want to find the best deal, which is a matter not simply of the exchange rate but of commission or bank charges. It can require a Treasury mandarin to work it all out but a calculator might do as an alternative. You might also think of taking some traveller's cheques, which are easily portable, easily turned into cash, and often redeemable if stolen, though you pay charges to have them issued and then exchanged.

Nowadays it always makes sense to obtain an internationally recognised credit card before you leave, if you don't have one already. In many countries, credit cards can be used to obtain cash, either over the counter in a bank or from an ATM or cash dispenser (the ones outside banks usually offer better value than the ones in stores). To use those, you will be required to obtain a code or PIN (personal identification number) for your card from your credit company to be able to get the cash and sometimes to validate purchases in shops. Credit cards are widely used for purchases in most developed countries and, though there have been recent concerns about their security, they still offer clear advantages over having to carry around large amounts of cash.

WHAT TO PACK

It is not difficult to decide what you will need to take with you, because it will probably be roughly the same as when packing at home for university. There is no point in taking too much. Globalisation means that most goods are available everywhere nowadays and often at similar prices. Obtaining goods abroad which are designed for the local climate may be more appropriate and even cheaper than bringing similar but less practical things from home. But you don't want to have to buy items you already have. Apart from clothes and study materials, which everybody takes, most of what you pack will be personal to you. Perhaps that is why those you consult will tell you that their life was saved by something as unlikely as a hot-water bottle or a hair lotion. But it may be possible to suggest a few more general rules, keeping local circumstances firmly in mind.

If you are moving to a warmer climate, light cotton clothing with plenty of pockets is the usual tip. If you are heading for somewhere colder, thick woollen outer clothing (sweaters, scarves, hats) may be useful items in your wardrobe. Both may be needed if your stay includes summer and winter. An umbrella is universally in vogue, either to keep off the rain or to shield you from the sun. You can generally forget about favourite foods because they will probably be available locally anyway, and customs regulations may prevent you from importing them. You can probably obtain most student supplies locally but you should certainly take anything to which you are particularly attached. If you have strong preferences among patent medicines, you should perhaps include some of those, but you will certainly find suitable local alternatives and, quite often, the originals, wherever you go.

COMPUTERS AND BOOKS

Many students have questions about computers. If you have a lap-top, do you take it with you or rely on what your host university can provide? Most students report that lap-tops are handy but not always essential. Many universities can provide you with computer access throughout the day and sometimes even into the night, though you should ask if you are in doubt. You also need to check on the compatibility of your computer with what is provided locally as there is clearly no point in taking something which may then be difficult to use. You will have to remember that electrical points and currents differ in different countries and you may need adaptors to get connected. The computer unit at your own university is likely to be informed and helpful if you are looking for advice. Taking security precautions to protect your computer (noting serial numbers, ensuring you have insurance cover) is also advisable.

Even though books are extremely heavy and are too burdensome to be carried abroad in bulk, you may have discovered which ones you will need to buy for your studies and found that you can save yourself some expense by obtaining them at home. If so, they can be taken with you or sent separately. If there are other books to which you are particularly wedded for your studies, you should of course consider including them in your luggage. A favourite dictionary can have an extra value abroad, for example. But, in general, you ought to anticipate that the books you require will all be available for purchase or in libraries abroad. You may not, in the end, take the courses you have been allocated and, as at home, it is unwise, without special guidance, to anticipate which particular books will be recommended for purchase or which will be of most use as the course proceeds.

PHOTOGRAPHS

It is quite likely that you will need a reasonable supply of passport-style photographs of yourself and it may make sense to get a supply before you go. Your host university will probably expect a couple of those and all sorts of other organisations will as well. If you are going to obtain student cards or rail passes, for example, photographs are often necessary as an attachment. Fortunately, they merely have to be a true likeness and not a work of art, so any local self-service photographic booth will produce acceptable ones. It might also help to get a few signed on the back by someone in authority, simply certifying that the likeness is genuine. Photo-ID is often required in countries outside Britain and, unless you are required to, it is not always safe to carry your passport around.

In many universities at home, you are now required to have a card which bears your photograph and the logo of the university on it and which also contains security features. It often doubles for use as a library card, a student services card and so on. This, too, can be taken with you. It may be out of date and may not serve the same purposes abroad but it provides evidence of who you are and indicates what you are doing. Those who don't have a university card can always get something made up locally with the photographs they have brought. A few students make their own name cards, containing their addresses at home and overseas, and with their photograph incorporated into it. If that is expensive, name cards without a photograph can be produced very cheaply (there are often machines in stations and airports which allow you to do this). They may be useful when introducing yourself to new friends but can seem pretentious to some and are less acceptable for identification purposes.

GIFTS

It is wise to pack some small presents which can be used as tokens of thanks in return for acts of hospitality or kindness. It is best to choose those typical of your own country or of your own university and those which are unlikely to be available locally (which is not as easy as it sounds: goods travel further and faster than people). Light, non-breakable, portable items, those which take up the least luggage space, are ideal, and that is presumably why most people end up getting a T-shirt with a logo on it. Despite what you hear or read, this is generally a perfectly acceptable gift, depending perhaps on quality, durability and country of origin – and attractive wrapping.

Some cultures require that presents should relate to the recipients and must indicate that you have given them special thought. Since you cannot always yet know who are to be the recipients, the alternative is to choose presents that instead reflect you and your identity and enthusiasms. They will then be appreciated as things that mean a lot to you and which you are hoping the recipient will also enjoy. If, in the event, they seem not to suit anyone, you can always, as an alternative, buy something locally and keep the presents for yourself!

ACADEMIC PREPARATION: COURSE SELECTION

One of the more important tasks which may face you before you leave is to make a preliminary selection of courses in the host institution. This may even be a requirement – it is normally part of the Learning Agreement for the Socrates/Erasmus programme, for example. It is often possible to obtain course information from prospectuses which are held by your home institution or by looking this up on the host institution's website. Your course adviser (and probably your Study Abroad office) at home should provide you with some indication of how many and what courses you must choose, and will indicate what they feel has worked best for others in your position in the past. If they don't, pester them until they do.

At this stage, of course, there are often no certainties. There is unlikely to be a guarantee that particular courses will actually be available once you arrive. All sorts of reasons (staff going on leave, the introduction of new courses) may prevent that. But if you and your academic adviser can agree on what might be appropriate from the information then available to you, it is generally easier to find something along the same lines and to make adjustments once you arrive. You may even be able to pre-book places on the Internet, which is enormously helpful and will save you from queues and delays. If you can communicate in advance about your requirements, it can certainly smooth the way. But you will be really lucky if everything can be arranged and decided in this way. In any case, some students say it is preferable to wait until after your arrival and to make your choices in the light of the latest information and the hot tips available only locally.

RESEARCHING THE INSTITUTION

It is worth doing some research to find out as much as you can about the institution you will be visiting before you get there. The Internet is an invaluable resource here and nowadays there are masses of information available on every institution. It can be especially helpful if you have to arrange your course choices on arrival to know something about the range on offer. It will also give you a clearer idea of the academic strengths of the place you are visiting because you will be able to see at a glance where its resources are clustered. It should also indicate where you should turn, as an international student, when you are looking for staff advice and support.

There are often Internet pages devoted to the services in the institution, such as the library, computer facilities and student activities. Again, it is worth spending a little time on those to ensure that you are aware of the similarities and differences between what you know from home and what you are likely to encounter abroad. If you have begun to research the place before you arrive, you will ask more pointed questions and be in a better position to understand the information you are given on arrival. You will also be better able to deal with practices unfamiliar to you, since you will have anticipated some of the problems to which they might give rise.

RESEARCHING THE AREA

You may also wish to get some books out of the library on the city or region where you will be living. It helps to know what there is to see and do, in the expectation that you will have enough free time to be able to benefit from this. One of the reasons for studying abroad is to get to know another country, so you should feel no guilt about devouring tourist travel literature. This often recommends that you read novels set in the country and a variety of academic works on things like local flora and fauna and geology, which are also of interest. The more you have begun to know about your host country and the more you reflect on this before your arrival, the more you are going to get out of the experience of living there.

It also helps to know something of the history and politics of your host country. Your fellow students will expect you to be reasonably interested in that and will probably want to tell you more. What you need is a framework into which you can fit the information that you pick up around you. You don't need to be an expert. Sounding as if you know it all already is something positively to avoid. But you do want to avoid giving offence by seeming wilfully ignorant, insensitive or chauvinistic.

TAKING A BREAK

Finally, it may be worth considering taking a break before you move to your new studies. However keenly you are looking forward to the time abroad, it can be a wrench to leave your family and familiar associations and set off into what it still perhaps the unknown. Giving yourself a small reward for your enterprise in the form of a short break before you start your studies can be a good way of allowing time to think yourself into your new role.

You may want to spend time with your friends and to go wherever you feel most relaxed. But many students prefer to take the break shortly after arriving and spend a week or so on an initial exploration of the city or country in which they are going to live. This gives them a chance to look round and gain first impressions as well to converse with locals and have experiences about which they can talk to their future fellow students. If no pre-term holiday is possible, it may be possible to pencil a short break in your diary for the first available opportunity thereafter. That tends to have a similar effect on your morale.

SUMMARY

Immediate preparations include:

- Initial accommodation and funds
- Packing
- Course selection
- Reading ahead
- Staying relaxed

SOME QUESTIONS

In preparing to go abroad, what have you decided to leave until last? How far can you prepare for your orientation into your new university before you leave home? What will you need to pack or send ahead and what can you reasonably hope to obtain more easily abroad?

11 ARRIVAL

'Train and bus times were on the Internet, so planning to get here was easy. But don't arrive on the holiday week-end.'

'Freshers' Week was beginning and we were still looking for a place to stay. We missed out on a lot of activities.'

With all the necessary arrangements made and the journey safely accomplished, you will be keen to begin your studies abroad. But even if you are an extremely experienced world traveller, being an international student can involve some surprises. The first few days of your time abroad can often be peculiarly puzzling as you try to discover where to find the things you need and what procedures you are meant to follow. The fact that you are dealing with regulations set down by governments and that these can seem threatening and onerous only adds to an air of doubt and uncertainty. But you do get through this, usually unscathed and often with your confidence enhanced. Each transaction accomplished, each obstacle surmounted make the next step easier. This chapter considers what you are likely to confront and suggests some ways of trying to cope.

IMMIGRATION

Provided that you have checked in advance, you should not have too many problems in entering another country as a student. You will obviously need to show your passport and it will be checked to ensure that it is up to date and valid for at least the length of your stay. It is a good idea to keep a separate note of your passport number, date of issue and expiry and visa number (if you have one), so that you have these with you whenever needed. If you need a residence permit, visa or admission document, you will have to present that, too. You will probably also require evidence for the immigration authorities that you are a bona fide student, which simply means being able to show them your certificate of eligibility or letter of admission from your host institution. You may be asked about your financial situation and may be expected to have a letter in your possession from a parent, grant authority or bank manager that can be used as evidence that you will be able to afford the costs of your programme.

Some countries have very elaborate regulations dealing with currency and will expect you to list all the money you have brought with you in cash and traveller's cheques. They may even issue you with a currency form, one copy of which must be retained carefully and handed in when you leave. If so, you will also have to record any money transfers which are made into your account while you are in the country, and keep all the documents concerned. It is best to have a folder for all this and to ensure that your records are up to date as it also serves to keep a check on your expenditure. Since the introduction of the internationally valid credit card, which makes it less necessary to hold ready cash, currency controls have generally been relaxed in most countries. Where they do still exist, you will have to take them very seriously or you will find yourself doing battle with the immigration authorities in order to be allowed to leave.

Health checks

It is also possible that you will be asked to complete a form about your general health. The intention, of course, is simply to decide whether or not you pose a risk of serious infection to others. Evidence for this is sometimes deduced from the fact that you have recently been in a country with a high incidence of some contagious illness. Outbreaks of highly infectious illnesses, like the recent SARS situation, do worry immigration officials. Their notions of geographical propinquity may also be rather looser than your own. An outbreak of infection anywhere within a thousand miles of the Britain may be enough to make them concerned. Some illnesses, such as meningitis, are also commonly thought of as affecting students particularly, so immigration authorities may harbour suspicions about you even if you have never had an illness in your life and are the very picture of the rudest good health.

If you have recently visited a country with a poor health record or if for any reason the United Kindom at the time you go abroad is suspected of harbouring some infectious illness, it might be sensible to have a word with your own GP before you leave. This at least gives you some ammunition with which to respond to questions. Your medical record in Britain is, of course, confidential to you and is not normally disclosed to anyone without your permission. But when entering another country, it is not improper for you to be asked, and you should be prepared to answer, general questions about your state of health. Although not at all likely under normal circumstances, the immigration authorities can demand that you be examined by one of their doctors before they admit you.

SEARCHING FOR ACCOMMODATION

If accommodation is not supplied and it has not been possible to arrange it in advance (despite your best efforts), your first requirement will be to find a place where you can lay your head at night. Alfresco arrangements are not recommended. There are usually desks at airports and stations where accommodation can be arranged but you need to be careful because these sometimes deal only with the expensive end of the market. If circumstances allow, it would be better to go immediately to your host institution and find the best source of advice on accommodation there. If this is not possible, you may have to rely on other expedients.

Finding temporary accommodation usually means seeking out a reasonably priced hotel or guest-house or lodgings. If you have a choice, it helps to be somewhere convenient for you to begin your search for permanent accommodation. But anywhere that looks safe and clean and convenient may do. It is always easier to find a place if you are clear about your requirements – how long will it take you to find a more permanent place, how much are you willing to pay for a temporary place, what kind of accommodation do you need while you search?

Finding long-term accommodation

Once you have found somewhere to stay for the time being, finding accommodation for the longer term will be the next object. Different countries and different cities have different circumstances, different ways of making known what is available and different rules about the conditions under which property is let. If you have obtained advice locally on how you should set about finding a place, particularly from your home and host universities, you are in a much better position to cope. Otherwise, if you know that students make use of a special housing agency or read the advertisements in a particular newspaper or use a designated website or a notice-board in a student building, you are going to cut out a lot of unnecessary work and worry. But searching can still take time. If your temporary accommodation is expensive, there is always a tendency to grasp at the first prospect of a more permanent place, which is obviously not advisable.

There are a few questions you should consider. Do you need to be near your institution? Is local transport convenient and cheap enough for you to live further away? Will this isolate you, socially? Are there areas where students traditionally concentrate? How do rents compare? The obligations you have to take on when renting property may be another issue. Being able to share with local students is often important. None of this is exactly straightforward. If you can search together with a friend, it helps enormously. You can then check with each other what has been said. Having company serves to keep your spirits up, too, when things don't go swimmingly. But searching in pairs isn't a good reason for dropping your guard. You still need to ask about the things that are important (price, safety, convenience, transport facilities, proximity of shops and so on).

OPENING A LOCAL BANK ACCOUNT

Wherever you are based, you need access to your funds fairly rapidly after your arrival. Some students don't open a bank account locally but rely on internationally recognised credit cards and on cash machines. The advantage of the latter is that you do not bring in too much, lose interest on your home account, and find yourself paying charges for converting the money into local currency when you arrive, and then back again into your own currency when you leave. But cash machines involve transaction charges, too, and they are often quite high. Opening a bank account may be better value but requires you to arrange for money transfers. They also have a cost and can be complicated to arrange. Usually they involve getting some sum to be sent to you on a regular basis, and it is hard to know initially exactly how much you will need. When you spend at a rate which differs from your calculations, periodic adjustments to the amount transferred may be necessary.

Opening an account locally is generally quite easy though there are exceptions. You usually need to bring along your passport and to have evidence of your address and other forms of identification. A local account gives you more certainty and more flexibility than trying to access your funds from home, and may be necessary, in any case, to pay for local costs such as your rent. But it has its problems, too. If you bring all your funds with you and put them into a local currency account, you are free from any volatility in exchange values. But that advantage may prove less convincing if your currency strengthens against the local one during your stay.

You also have access to your funds immediately the transfer is cleared (which may still take a few weeks) and can then get easy access to cash. Sometimes with an account you are also entitled to a local credit card or cheque-book which may be more widely acceptable locally than international cards. But unexpected bank charges and deductions often arise. In the end, you have to decide for yourself which arrangement suits your situation best and seems least costly or inconvenient.

REGISTERING AS A RESIDENT

In some cases, as a temporary resident in a new country, you will be required to register with the local civic authorities. Your host university will tell you about it if it applies in your case. Most students find it bureaucratic and intrusive though they are often unaware that those coming to the United Kingdom face similar requirements. It is obviously better if you can convince yourself that the process has some point. It does mean that your presence is recorded and that the law recognises your right to be there. It is best done straight away as many other things can depend on it. When registering locally, it may also be a good idea at the same time to make your arrival known to the British embassy or consulate if there is one nearby. Now and then, UK officials may want to talk to British students and, to do this, they need to know where you are. They may even invite you to some function if they know you are around. A short note explaining who you are and how long you will stay and offering to give advice to anyone enquiring about studying in Britain will probably go down quite well.

Registration with the state or regional or local government is not often required these days. If it is, it will have a cost and will certainly take time, as you usually have to report personally. You will also be expected to bring along some documents which make it clear who you are and what you are doing. Your passport is probably essential and, once more, the admission letter from your host institution will prove valuable. You will also be expected to have a permanent address or to give a temporary address and then return later with a more permanent one. You are normally supposed to keep the authorities informed if you change address in the course of your stay but you can sometimes do that by letter rather than in person.

PERSONAL SAFETY

Safety is a major consideration for international students and for their universities. When incidents do occur where a student has been placed in danger, there is always an inquiry and an attempt to ensure that extra safeguards are provided for the future. In serious cases, students have even been withdrawn from a particular city or country because it is felt unsafe for them to remain. But it is very hard to make provision for what is, of its nature, unpredictable. You can often discover if an area has a very high incidence of crime but this is not a certain guide. Some of the world's leading universities are situated in, or close to, problem areas but security is tight there and few of their students feel in the least unsafe. Equally, even if you have chosen an institution within an area notoriously safe and generously policed, you may still find yourself witnessing, or being the victim of, a crime. The likelihood of your being involved in anything of that sort is, of course, remote. Yet students are known to be victims of choice for some kinds of petty criminals, and cases are recorded where harassment or even physical assaults have taken place.

What can you do to avoid danger or to protect yourself without making yourself feel anxious or unsafe? The problem is obviously greatest in the first few weeks when you are unfamiliar with your new environment. You need initially to protect your valuables, locking them away if that is possible. You should not be seen in public places displaying large amounts of cash or jewellery. There is usually safety in numbers and it is wise to keep to well-populated streets and to avoid those that appear deserted. You should prefer the longer but more brightly lit route to your destination to the quicker but darker one. If you are moving around after dark, you may be wise to choose a taxi (particularly if you can share with one or two others) rather than walking or taking little-used public transport. Above all, you have to give a little more thought to safety than you would do at home, even if you believe that you are in a safer environment. Experience is the great guide. After a time, by observing others, you may decide to relax some or all of your special precautions. But, by then, you will presumably have good reasons for doing so, because you are sure that others are doing the same.

TIME DIFFERENCES

Nearly everyone going abroad from Britain enters a different time zone. Time difference can become a concern, if only that it has to be remembered when phoning home. If the difference is only an hour or two, you may also find at first that you get hungry or tired before (or after) the locals do but it won't normally be very disconcerting, though this depends partly on the distance you have travelled. Those going to France or Germany will be very little affected; those going to South Africa may be rather more so. When you travel due east or due west and the time difference is large, nearly everyone experiences what is called jet lag. This is a major problem for the modern world when so many business people spend much of their lives gadding about between one continent and another. There have been innumerable studies of jet lag, all of which suggest ways of tackling the problem. None of them works. There is an old joke that runs: I am suffering from insomnia but am trying to sleep it off. Those suffering from jet lag may have to be content with the same approach.

The effects of time difference range from the mild to the severe. In a severe case, you will find it difficult to concentrate during the day and will often feel overwhelmed by waves of tiredness. During the night, when you want to go to sleep, you will find yourself wide awake and ready for a party. These are dangerous signs because you are unlikely in this condition to be able to study effectively and may be so forgetful and unaware that you miss appointments or lose valuables. The advice you are usually given is to try to stay out in the sun (or at least the daylight) for as long as you can in your first few days abroad. This allows your eyes to inform your brain that you are in a different time zone. You should also watch your diet, drink more water than normal and avoid coffee and cola. Doctors also talk about the need for sleep hygiene. You should try to encourage yourself into sleep in the evening by relaxing more and more as bedtime approaches and gradually and consciously winding down. Deliberate efforts of this kind seem to help. But, in the end, only time cures a problem that time created, and it may take a fortnight or even longer before you begin to feel entirely back to normal.

CONTACTING HOME

It is important that you phone, text or e-mail home soon after your arrival, not only to reassure your family that you are safe and well and that the journey has been completed, but also to reassure yourself that keeping in touch is not going to be difficult. These days, it is usually quite simple to arrange for your mobile phone to be used abroad or for you to obtain a new mobile for use when abroad. You may need advice about costs and options, and you should be able to get this from any reputable dealer. The mobile, needless to say, also needs to be kept safely when abroad and should not be flourished too publicly. In some places it may be cheaper and just as easy to use public telephones, so you need to enquire about that, too. Phone cards can cut telephone costs and you may be able to discover which is the cheapest for phoning Britain. Your university may well provide you with access to e-mail facilities and you can use those to keep in touch if you've made the necessary preparations. There is usually no shortage of ways of keeping in touch. But, now and then, you may, in the middle of your various diversions, have to make an effort to summon up the will.

Realising how easy it is to keep in touch is a way of making you feel more relaxed. But, primarily, making contact with home also has a practical benefit. You should certainly let someone in your university know that you have arrived so that this can be recorded. If any details of your accommodation or courses have still to be decided, you should also let someone know what those are at the earliest opportunity. Because, in your time abroad, you remain a home student, it is important that your university should be able to contact you easily. You should provide as many of your contact details as you can. You may not get a reply immediately but you can be sure that the information has been noted and that it will be used to get back to you when the occasion arises.

SUMMARY

On arrival, you should be prepared to deal with:

- Immigration authorities
- Health checks
- Settling into accommodation
- Getting local currency
- Coping with time differences
- Keeping safe
- Contacting home

SOME QUESTIONS

How far can you prepare for the things you will do on arrival? What do you need to have with you on the journey to get through immigration smoothly? What addresses and phone numbers will you need to have searched out and kept with you?

12 REGISTRATION

'Getting registered was a nightmare. Stay calm. It seems absolute chaos but it works in the end.'

'Make sure you take all your paperwork with you everywhere. Ask lots of questions and try to go early and beat the queues.'

No subject seems to create such annoyance for students as registration. Whether this is a problem of those abroad or simply a problem is less clear. Different practices overseas, different bureaucratic bodies, different personnel, different expectations and different timings may simply complicate further what is already complicated enough. This chapter may help keep down your blood pressure.

USING UNIVERSITY SERVICES

Many universities abroad are larger than those in Britain and so can appear intimidating, amorphous. But, in most cases, arrangements will have been made for you to have a particular contact, an initial entry point, within your host institution. This is often a Study Abroad office or Student Exchange office where specialist staff are employed to deal with your problems. Sometimes it is a student union used by all students, home as well as overseas, and it is expected that staff will be able to help both. In other cases, it may all be left to your department or school where staff who help to run the exchanges or international study arrangements may be assigned to keep an eye on your needs and welfare. Sometimes each international student is attached to an adviser and you are told about this in your joining instructions. If you have not been given any indication about what point of contact you should use, it may be necessary to enquire. Usually the admissions office would be the best place to start.

Having someone to turn to when you arrive in a new institution is enormously valuable and it is worth spending time cultivating a few other contacts as well. Don't hesitate to search out people, if you think they can be useful, and make yourself known. Compared to most other university systems, the British one offers quite a close degree of supervision for students. Elsewhere, the structures are often looser or less formal though, as ever, you must also be prepared to find the opposite. If you have established to whom to refer matters at home when decisions have to be taken about your studies, your main need initially at your host institution is for someone to advise on the structures and rules there. That is not something that many lecturers feel able to handle unless they have been specially assigned to do so. But there are always individuals within each institution who are experts on such matters, particularly when dealing with international students and, once you identify them, you can take your concerns there.

OBTAINING ACADEMIC ADVICE

Compared to full-degree study, Study Abroad requires you to make a very rapid adjustment to your new environment. The fact that the time you have abroad is short, an academic year or less, and that the studies have to be fitted into the structures of your host university as well as those at home makes the need to settle down quickly important. It helps, of course, that you have probably begun your preparations and perhaps even made a preliminary selection of courses before you left home. But, once you arrive, the preparations have to intensify. Like soldiers jumping from a helicopter on to a battlefield, you have to 'hit the ground running'.

Getting signed up for classes is one of your first major tasks. It can be simple if you have been given instructions on how to find your academic adviser, and it can be a pain ('a premonition of hell', one student found) when you are wandering around lost. As in the United Kingdom, you will find that there are secretaries and administrators with responsibilities for particular fields of study. You have to find the ones in the area that interests you and then ask for advice. Initially you may also have to be patient and persistent. Everyone is very busy at the start of the academic year. It is likely that information is provided somewhere about the courses available (a booklet, a notice-board, on-line?) and the contact addresses for enquiries. Once you find that, the way forward often opens up immediately. If you can't find the addresses or if the people listed are hopeless, you may have to follow the crowd or rely on what others tell you.

LOCAL COURSE SELECTION

When your course selection is decided long in advance there is nothing further to do on arrival except register. But most students will probably have to make some choices locally. It would be ideal if you had agreed a list of possibles with your academic adviser at home and could now firm this up after questioning your new student colleagues. They don't know your interests and requirements but they have an up-to-date knowledge of what seems popular or highly regarded among local students and what is not. Unfortunately, there is usually little time for consultation as even they are particularly busy when term starts. In any case, places are usually in limited supply and you often feel obliged to grab what you can get.

Those left to choose courses on their own should already have drawn up a plan. This now needs to be adapted to what is available and to what fits with your requirements. Selecting courses in the light of what previous students from your university have advised is not a bad policy. Sometimes the best technique is to try to blend tradition and novelty, moving forward the studies you have already begun at home but also exploring new avenues and prospects. Where it proves possible, it can be a good idea to take a course that relates to the country in which you have come to live. This can be challenging. Local students already have a far greater background knowledge than you are likely to have. You may be well advised to seek advice about which particular course would be most suitable. But the gains in studying some aspect of local life while also observing it are real.

COURSE ENTRY

If you strike it lucky, you will be given immediate access to all your first choices and may even be able to try them out and 'drop and add' courses in the first couple of weeks. Much more commonly, you'll find that places are limited and you will have to make a case to become accepted. In many universities this means getting your selection approved by the relevant course tutors before you can register. It may involve you in a lengthy campaign, moving from redoubt to redoubt (or at least from office to office), with small advances secured or reverses suffered along the way. To do this, you obviously have to have reserves as well as first choices in mind, and you may find yourself 'waitlisted' (i.e. put on a waiting list). In the end, you'll win through (or at least have a set of courses that looks distinctly appealing) provided you capitalise on your assets. You have to be prepared to sell yourself. You must be blunt in suggesting that international students deserve special consideration, insistent that the course is required for some study purpose at home, and downright importunate in indicating that you are obviously the ideal candidate for the class. This may not come naturally at first. If it does, you should resolve immediately to consider a career in sales promotion.

Most students recommend that you try to arrange all your courses very quickly, ideally within one day. Of course, it is important that your final programme is one about which you feel confident. For all the hassle, there is generally a good deal of support for international students, particularly those on exchanges, wherever you go, and you will probably find that that wins you favours. If you can get everything done quickly, you will certainly feel more settled and more prepared to tackle less bureaucratic but equally vital necessities, such as eating and sleeping. You must also remember that you require permission from your academic adviser at home for the final selection you make. This gives you an opportunity to consult about anything else that is causing you concern.

UNIVERSITY REGISTRATION

The process of registration can be another hurdle and it can also be purely routine, particularly if you get help or advice. Sometimes, you will be on your own and puzzled by the differences between the system at home and the one you've encountered abroad. Many students complain that the bureaucracy involved in registration abroad feels interminable, like watching Big Brother. In some cases, it seems to involve them in visiting several different offices (all with different times of opening), obtaining multiple signatures, securing endorsement stamps and having identity checks. If that is your experience, you've probably got a full house. But there are no prizes. The only sensible thing to do is to grin and bear it. Console yourself with the thought that it's doing them more harm than it is you.

You can also try to turn it to your advantage. Some students find that conversations struck up in registry queues are the beginnings of lifelong friendships. You can also use it to get to know the institution, particularly if you are required to travel all over the campus. But beware of the request for the missing document, which always puts you back to the end of the queue. Some people recommend that you should get a file and put into it every document that you could conceivably ever need, from your birth certificate to your bus ticket, just so that you know you can always produce what is required. Take the file with you everywhere, and you'll probably beat the system.

BEING CLEAR

In your first days in any new institution, the possibility of getting things wrong is very high. When you are operating in a second language (or just in a second version of English) you may even find it difficult to follow what is being said. It is very important that you recognise that you need to understand any instructions you are given and have a right to expect that you should. If you are coping with a new language or an unfamiliar accent, some misunderstandings are almost inevitable. It may mean that you have to repeat your question when the first response you get is unclear, and to go on repeating it till you are sure. Of course, this has to be done politely and preferably with a smile. But it has to be done.

Because you are excited and perhaps unsure about what to expect, you may also find it a problem at first to absorb everything you are told. Written instructions are easier in this respect but may not always be available. The solution is probably to try to meet other international students as quickly as you can and begin to compare notes with them. By checking your version of what was said against theirs, you may begin to feel more confident about what is expected of you. There is always strength in numbers. If you and your fellow international students can go as a group to ask for clarification and advice, for example, your request will be given more time and usually more consideration.

ATTENDING ORIENTATION

Many universities offer an orientation programme for new international students. These last from an evening up to week and sometimes then include occasional events held over an entire semester. If you want to attend (you may even be required to) you have to arrive at the appropriate time. Study Abroad students often feel equivocal about attending orientations. After all, you are not a new student and much that is communicated at orientations is designed for those who are new to university. You may also resent the time it takes and the cost.

But the gains for those who do attend orientation are usually considerable. There are almost always sessions on the institution, the locality and such basic matters as transport and security, for example, which those from abroad are likely to find useful. Many sessions will be specifically for the benefit of international students (perhaps all of them if there are enough of you) and are a means for you to begin the process of acculturation. Sessions exclusively for international students are particularly appreciated as they allow you to meet others from overseas before you have to tackle the challenge of meeting the locals. Almost every student who attends an orientation comments on how valuable the social contacts proved to be.

MAKING FRIENDS

As a Study Abroad student, you are at a slight disadvantage in trying to make friends with local students. Most of them will have begun their university study while you were in Britain. By the time you arrive, they will have built up a circle of friends with whom they feel comfortable and at ease. You are, by their standards, a latecomer. You are also known to be someone who will disappear back to Britain after only a comparatively short time which makes the effort of making friends with you rather less of an investment. Of course, if you have a dazzling personality, great charm and devastating social skills, you will overcome all obstacles. But most of us find that we have to be rather more active and assertive in making friends than at home.

One way round the obstacle is to turn first to others in the same boat. There will probably be many other students studying abroad temporarily and they will be as anxious as you to find company. The trouble is that this can lead to the 'ghetto' mentality when overseas students become absorbed in one another and become totally isolated from local students. If you begin by getting to know other overseas students (with whom initially you will have a great deal to talk about and to compare experiences with) you ought to try to break through into friendships with the locals, too. You have to find ways of doing this. Joining in sports or in some student activity, such as choir singing or politics, is one obvious route. Sitting next to someone in lectures and then suggesting going for coffee together is another. Obviously being sensitive to your position as a visitor and guest is a necessary element in how you make friends. Not being discouraged when your first efforts are not rewarded is important, too. In Britain, pubs play a big role in student socialising. This is likely to be less true elsewhere. But student cafés and bistros often serve the same purpose.

SUMMARY

On arrival, you need to give thought to:

- Registering as a resident
- Getting academic advice
- Finalising your programme

You need also to think about:

- Understanding instructions
- Attending orientation
- Making friends

SOME QUESTIONS

Can you find out when, where and how you register as a student? Can you find out when, where and how you register for courses? Which of these processes comes first? What opportunities do you have for checking this information with others?

13 STUDY SKILLS: THE REQUIREMENTS

'There was a lot of class participation in lectures. The work was not too hard but there were large volumes of required reading and lots of exams.'

'Lectures lasted up to three hours with no class participation, and assessment consisted only of a presentation in front of a lecture audience, a few short papers and a fifteen minute oral.'

Mastering new teaching and learning styles is not something with which you are likely to be entirely unfamiliar. Moving from school to university almost always involves a much bigger challenge than moving from your home to an overseas university. But undoubtedly there will be differences between the teaching methods you are used to in the United Kingdom and those you encounter abroad. To give a good account of yourself, you will have to adjust to these changes and surmount them. Unfortunately, the variety of styles is so great that it is difficult to give advice. This chapter looks at some of the most likely challenges and considers how you might best meet them.

THE LEARNING CYCLE

Most students abroad encounter some differences in teaching or learning styles. This can often be welcome but not if it is unexpected and problematic. A few students say that the experience of having to cope with a different style initially unnerved them so much that they felt de-skilled and depressed. The knowledge and understanding they had earlier acquired of how to study and how to be successful now seemed suddenly not to work. Sometimes even very able students are so affected by discovering that study methods are different that they begin to lose confidence. Such a catastrophic reaction is no doubt an extreme one. But less severe responses of puzzlement and confusion are not all that unusual. In the first few weeks of studying abroad, most students, when in class, feel a little disoriented.

If things don't improve or if, as time goes on, your marks or grades are less good than you expected, you may even find yourself having to learn to study again from scratch. Sociologists call this process 'the learning cycle', something, they claim, nearly everyone experiences to some degree when making major intellectual adjustments, such as moving from school to university. An initial excitement at encountering study methods which are unusual or different can often give way to growing doubts about your ability to cope with them. At this point, you can worry so much that a sense of crisis develops and some even contemplate giving up altogether. After a little time most people sense that they are beginning to recover. Your confidence starts to grow again and you gradually return to an awareness of being in control. Unfortunately, this learning cycle is no easier – though it is probably no more difficult either – if you have to experience it abroad. But it is not certain that you will be affected in this way. Many people take to different study methods like ducks to water and thrive on the challenges they present.

LEARNING STYLES

Adapting learning styles to suit a new situation is not generally unfamiliar to most students. In fact, the styles of learning you use are normally quite diverse and are adjusted almost unconsciously once you have decided which would be most suitable for the task in hand. At each stage of your studies, you probably try out new methods and relearn older ones. The differences may be subtle but, if you think back to your first year and note how much more assured you have become as a student, you will realise how far you have travelled. You don't lose these skills by going abroad. But being abroad can make the effort of relearning seem more evident and therefore more conscious. There is a tendency to blame 'the system' for forcing you to change rather than seeing change as an opportunity for the further development of your growing learning skills, something that you should find will be of lasting use and benefit.

If at first you are concerned, it can help to know in advance that many students have problems initially. But it is also important that you take early steps to begin to adapt your learning strategies. When the solution is not obvious, you will probably need advice – from the teaching staff or from your fellow students. You have to take steps to discover in particular what is being looked for as evidence of mastery in your subject and how success is measured. Once that is clearer, you will begin to appreciate how your armoury of skills might be best deployed. It is usually only when you remain uncertain about what is required over a long period that your confidence is threatened.

ADAPTING TO CHANGE

When you start your studies abroad, one of the first things you must establish from your fellow students and your lecturers is what work is expected of you. Do you have to attend lectures, tutorials, individual meetings with academic staff, laboratory classes, practicals? What is required, what is encouraged, what is entirely optional? Some students advise attending classes even when they are not a requirement or even when locals habitually cut them. They see this as a means of negating the charge, which is sometimes made, that Study Abroad students are less committed or less conscientious about their studies than degree students. It also ensures that you come to know the teaching staff better which can help, particularly when it comes to assessment.

Once you have deduced how the work demands differ from those that you are familiar with in the United Kingdom, you will then find it easier to make the necessary adjustments. But it can still take a little time. If there are many more requirements and rules than at home, for example, some students can at first feel spoon fed and denied choice. On the other hand, if there are far fewer requirements than at home, others may be equally unhappy, convinced that the instruction is insufficient and that they are not being given clear guidance. Not everyone, of course, responds to change like this. Some people like having more guidance in their work and others feel more respected and more in control of their own learning by having less. It is just that most of us expect the familiar and take time to adjust emotionally to being required to change to something different.

LABORATORY WORK AND INDIVIDUAL LEARNING

In the pure and applied sciences and in some of the social sciences, learning abroad can involve a good deal of laboratory, group work and self-learning. This is not necessarily unfamiliar – in Britain, these techniques often feature more strongly in later years of study. But the emphasis may be different. In the rest of Europe particularly, science students often remark that they have been given access to more advanced classes than at home, including postgraduate ones. The intention is usually that they should be allowed to work on research projects alongside the local academic staff. Though challenging, the students often see this as beneficial, not least linguistically (in that any deep knowledge of the local language is much less likely to be necessary) and socially (in that relations with fellow researchers are likely to be quite relaxed and personal) as well, of course, as academically.

But no two laboratories are run in precisely the same manner, and you may find yourself having to adapt your skills. The degree of supervision involved, for example, will vary. You may also find that being required to work more often in a group means being able to negotiate, co-operate and pool your knowledge, something clearly at variance with much of the individualist and competitive tradition of studies in Britain. Getting used to another laboratory also involves getting used to different work practices, different times of work, different methods and different attitudes. If you are prepared for this from the start, it can make things much easier.

INDIVIDUAL TUITION AND SEMINARS

In many courses abroad, what proves striking is that individual tuition, student-centred group work, such as seminars, and private study are mainly employed. Individual tuition is more personal than a lecture course but generally involves less frequent contact with the staff. Tutors certainly won't be able to see you individually as often as you would expect to see teaching staff at lectures. But when you do see them your contact is likely to be much more intensive. They expect you directly to raise with them any problems you are having in understanding the material. They look to you in part to suggest an agenda for the meetings, deriving from your reading, the work you have been set or are setting yourself, and any written work on which you are engaged. When only infrequent contact with tutors is possible, you have to discipline yourself more firmly and ensure that you are working regularly and systematically on your own. This may involve you in devising and following a strict timetable of work and setting yourself specific tasks which you should agree with the tutor at each meeting. It probably helps if you keep a kind of diary and note what work you have done and what items you would like to discuss.

Where group work forms the basis of a course, a premium is put on a different set of skills. You will find that you need to be able to express yourself verbally and to engage in debate. You will have to be able to get the subject up from the recommended reading and then use the class discussion to ensure that you have grasped its essentials and begun to explore some of its ramifications. Establishing a work routine for yourself is obviously more important – perhaps crucial – when the supervision is less personal. Regular group meetings assist you to develop that but they also require you to put in a definite amount of reading (not necessarily exhaustive) on what needs to be a very regular basis.

LEARNING FROM LECTURES

One of the differences in teaching abroad most often commented upon lies in the attention given to lectures, though this is generally truer for students in the humanities than the sciences and may be truer of North America than of some countries in Europe. You can find you have lectures daily in every subject. You may be expected to attend every lecture or to provide reasons why you have not done so. Records are sometimes kept. You may be expected to ask questions or make points in the course of the lecture. Failure to do so may be taken as evidence of lack of interest or of academic difficulty. You may have to note down a great deal of the information conveyed and what you are told in lectures may form the basis of your examinations. In some cases, you are required to prepare for every lecture by doing assigned reading in advance and you may be asked questions during the lecture to check that you have done so. Your understanding of lectures may be tested frequently, perhaps in weekly or even daily tests. If this is what you confront and it is unfamiliar to you, you do need to be able to cope.

Most people do so quite readily. Lectures are important enough in Britain for adaptation to be relatively automatic. By the time you go abroad, you will have been given a good deal of practice in listening to lectures, taking notes and making use of what you learn for essays and exams or tutorials and practicals. You may even be familiar with lectures in which you are expected to ask questions or offer opinions occasionally (that's probably what some tutorials feel like). The main problem is likely to be in adjusting to the weight of lecturing. You may also find it harder to take notes in a situation in which questioning by the class is habitually a major element, particularly if the discussion wanders. Giving lecture notes a greater prominence in determining what and how you learn can also be a hurdle. But the solution is probably mainly a matter of adjusting your study time to suit. Most students who have to adjust to learning mainly from lectures say that they spend far more time on class-work preparation than they would at home. As a result, they often feel that they have to work harder, but nearly all conclude that it is not as demanding intellectually.

OPTIONAL LECTURES

In some countries, lectures are merely an optional supplement to individual learning. This is often the case where separate arrangements are made for international students and the lectures provided are those open to everyone. In such cases, it is often up to you to decide whether these would be helpful or not. Those who choose to are free to ignore them. This situation also involves you in making study adjustments. It imposes on you the obligation of deciding whether you are likely to gain more by going to the lectures than by reading on your own, and it requires you to decide how much your understanding of a subject relates to your attendance at lectures.

That may depend in part on how well the lecturer communicates or what you feel you are gaining from the lectures. It may depend on how important you find it to have what lectures provide: a formally arranged – as opposed to a self-imposed – routine to mark out and guide you in your studies. And it may depend on how far the content of the lectures matches your principal interests. But dispensing with lectures altogether, when any are offered, does involve risks. Lectures are very good at providing you with an indication of the sorts of things you need to know in order to master a course, and they suggest what subjects you need to cover and in what depth. It is often harder to pick up such information on your own. On the other hand, even at home you may already have the option of deciding whether or not to attend lectures and so feel entirely relaxed about confronting the same decision abroad.

LECTURES AND LECTURE NOTES

Where lectures are given central prominence, it would be wise to look again at your skills in note taking. How good are you at recording the gist of a lecture in notes? What do you find helps most to impress the content of a lecture on your mind? Is it useful to read a round the lecture, studying ahead in anticipation and then consolidating what you have learned by some selective supplementary reading afterwards? Does it help to structure your notes? If lecture notes are provided by the lecturer, is it useful to annotate these rapidly with the information you would most like to retain? Are there recommended textbooks for the course, and in what ways can they be deployed as a supplement to the lectures? Are you expected to use lecture time to clarify points about which you are uncertain and which at home you would normally have reserved for tutorials?

If lectures are acknowledged as central, you clearly will have to spend more time on them, deciding what needs to be committed to memory most and what is purely illustrative. You will have to try actively to relearn what you have absorbed in them – by highlighting key steps in an argument, by summarising points of detail, by reshaping the whole so that it fits into a framework that makes sense to you. You will have to decide how much time needs to be devoted to this. It cannot be so much that it distracts you from your other commitments but must be enough for it to be done regularly and routinely. To prepare for examinations, you will also have to decide which topics seemed most interesting to you and which you feel you could now explain to the examiners most convincingly.

CONTACTING STAFF

Another difference you may find abroad lies in the availability of teaching staff to assist you with your learning outside lectures. In Britain, where tutorials are widely employed, you usually set up appointments with staff individually only as the need arises. Abroad, particularly in North America, you may find such meetings are much more expected and routine. The lecturing staff and their assistants may hold regular 'office hours' when they are available to discuss your progress, particularly in essays or projects which you have been assigned. British students sometimes find this practice odd (it probably seems like currying favour) and are reluctant to take advantage of it. Those who do, however, rapidly appreciate its value. The staff holding office hours are often the ones employed to grade your assessed work. Talking things over with them in advance allows you to be clear about what they are looking for and what they expect of you, which can be enormously helpful.

On the other hand, some students abroad, especially in some European countries, complain about teaching staff who are impossible to find, excessively formal, excessively casual, or downright unhelpful. It may be that a different method of learning is being expected in that case, one in which you have to assume greater responsibility yourself for what you learn. It helps to talk over this assumption with your fellow students and perhaps with an adviser at home or abroad to ensure that you are still on the right track and are not misunderstanding a situation which has left you puzzled or uncertain. Once you are sure you know the routine, it is again much easier to adapt.

LEARNING STYLES

It is often suggested that a chief characteristic of education in the United Kingdom is that it encourages a measure of open debate and a questioning of 'authorities'. By contrast, it is argued, older cultures (those of East Asia are usually cited) are more likely to emphasise respecting and assimilating the views of the principal authorities. Some UK students in countries abroad also get the impression that showing respect for the views of their fellow students in tutorials is more highly valued than demonstrating an ability to challenge or question them. Neither of these impressions is necessarily correct. There are various forms of academic discourse which are thought appropriate in different situations in different countries. When abroad, you may initially find the ways in which academic authorities and students are interrogated unfamiliar and perhaps unconvincing. But there is a danger of confusing style and substance. Different rules on politeness may mean that different forms of interrogation are being employed. Politeness, however, does not necessarily imply agreement. You need to be patient at the beginning and try to find out how agreement, disagreement and doubts are expressed in the local culture. It may not be quite the same as at home.

Students in countries where more face-to-face confrontation is common can also be uncertain about what is required. You may find that the locally approved form of discourse is far more aggressive than you are used to, and you may even feel that there seems to be a lack of respect for the authorities and that this makes you uncomfortable. Your observations may be sound, but it is more likely that the differences relate to different styles of debate and discussion. If you are going to learn from your tutors and fellow students, as you must, then some attempt to understand their perspective and to follow the ways in which they express themselves is clearly necessary. That certainly requires effort and it probably requires experience. Of course, it is not always necessary or desirable for you to allow this to affect your style of learning. Differences can be valuable. Being aware of the possibility of difference is the first step on the way to understanding. Trying to appreciate why any difference exists is the second. Deciding whether the difference has such significance that it needs to be absorbed is the third.

PAIR BONDING

When studying in another country, it often helps enormously if you can have a 'pair' to talk to, a local student willing to compare impressions with you. Some universities arrange this for you. But it is also something you can try and foster for yourself. Finding someone who shares your academic interests and who would like to know more about study in the United Kingdom is usually the best approach. You can then try to meet socially on some casual basis, perhaps over tea or coffee, and use those occasions to discuss how you are finding your studies. The advantage is that you can often be more frank with a fellow student than you might want to be with an academic, and it may be easier to admit to your difficulties in understanding local attitudes or practices.

It also helps a bit if you are in touch with someone else from your own country willing to share experiences with you. In a wish to be part of the local society, we sometimes neglect to keep in touch with students from home. There are good reasons not to do that. When two of you are sharing experiences and have the same background, you can gain much comfort from realising that your concerns are common. It helps you to separate what is individual from what seems to be systematic and so puts you in a better position to find solutions. It is also easier to assimilate something from a new culture if you do not feel that this puts you at risk of losing your own. By having friends from home while abroad, you tend to be more relaxed and at ease about your own identity, which makes it less challenging to try out new ones. As mentioned, the danger is in only having friends from home.

ENDURING LANGUAGE PROBLEMS

If you are studying in a second language and you are not totally fluent, improving your language skills may require some of the time which at home you might devote to learning other things. Nearly all academic communication involves language (though gesture and body language feature as well). Everything hinges on your being able to make yourself understood. At the sophisticated level required by university study, there is always the possibility of falling short. No doubt your tutors will make some allowance for this but, if they or your fellow students are uncertain about what you have said, there are limits to what they can allow. Theoretically, because you were presumably required to reach some standard in the language before being accepted for study abroad, the problem should not be deep. But, if it does arise, you need to deal with it.

When a language difficulty becomes marked and begins to affect your academic success, it can undermine your confidence and make you feel stressed or despondent. Sadly, it is often felt most keenly near the start of your studies when you are at your most vulnerable. The sensible reaction is to seek help, within your institution initially. You may be able to form self-help groups with other international students, or your institution may have its own suggestions. Once your ability grows and confidence returns, you need not continue with this. But, if the difficulty persists and proves serious, you may have to undertake a course in language improvement, externally if necessary, though what you can do has to be balanced against the time available and competing commitments.

ESSAYS AND PROJECTS

Writing essays and projects generally involve fewer problems of adjustment. In the United Kingdom, you are allowed a specified time to prepare them. You are normally given guidance on reading and an indication of how long your essay or report should be. Suggestions are generally offered about the formalities you must observe (such as footnoting or providing a bibliography). Even if the rules abroad turn out to be different, you have the bases there for determining how you must respond. You need first to note the amount of preparation time you have been allowed and from this you should be able to decide what coverage – reading or research – you can reasonably be expected to provide. Secondly, you need to follow precisely the instructions you have been given. Sometimes you will find that what you are being asked to do differs from what you expected at first. But different formats apply everywhere. Thirdly you may need to know what preparation is considered appropriate: do you bring in new materials or rely only on the ones provided, for example? Finally, you must discover how your response should be presented and how long it should be.

Where advice is not routinely on offer, it is sometimes difficult to seek it out, particularly if other students seem able to cope without it. But as an international student, you will usually find that asking advice is not seen as unwelcome even if you have to steel yourself to do it. Academics know what they want you to achieve but are often uncertain about what you need to know to get there. They tend to prefer you to try out something so that they can comment on what you have done. This can be less helpful to those coming from outside the system who may be aiming at something else rather than failing to achieve what was expected. If you have an opportunity to talk over in advance with a tutor the requirements for written work, you should certainly take it. If not, it can be useful to create an opportunity to do it once your first work has been assessed.

EXAMINATIONS

Like projects and essays, examinations can mean different things in different settings, at home and abroad. If you are examined much more frequently than in Britain, you may feel under great pressure but will soon realise that examinations are not so arduous. Sometimes in the United Kingdom the word 'test' is used for intermediate periodic assessments and 'examinations' for 'finals'. If you are used to tests at home, more frequent examinations abroad will occasion no great concern. You will be aware that test preparation is likely to relate to more directed reading and to be more dependent on memorisation than with 'finals'. For tests, the favoured style is usually 'surface learning', concentrating more on being able to explain, clearly and accurately, what you have heard or read.

On the other hand, if you are not examined until the end of the course and are then asked to produce something like a thesis, you will have to display the different skills of 'deep learning' and show that your time has been productively engaged throughout. You must not only have spent time reading among the recommended literature, but you must have pondered the problems discussed and formed your own views about which issues seem important. That will require you to have taken notes from your reading throughout and to have begun to assemble your thoughts into an argument. The argument will set out the problem, illustrate how it has been viewed by different scholars and bring evidence to bear for each point you wish to make. It will also draw the points together in a conclusion. Yet deep learning and surface learning are not entirely different categories. Both involve balancing evidence with argument, reading with reflection, assertions with quotations, facts with speculation.

METHODS OF ASSESSMENT

Another area where differences can emerge is in the marking of scripts. At home, British students are told that they are being marked against some standard which is objectively established. Quite commonly, assessed work will be marked by more than one examiner (and perhaps by external examiners) to ensure that this standard is evenly maintained across the class (and between institutions). Abroad, students often discover that an individual tutor has much more independence in undertaking assessments. Where the assessment is derived from multiple-choice questions or computerised testing that hardly matters. Where it involves lengthy essays or projects, it can seem, to those used to the British system, worryingly subjective.

Concern is caused, too, when a lecturer announces that the course will be marked on a mathematical basis relating to the class as a whole. The favourite is usually the bell curve chart, whereby perhaps 10 per cent of the class will have high marks and 10 per cent low marks, 20 per cent will have marks just below or just above those, and everyone else will have marks in the lower middle range. The idea is, of course, to emphasise class competitiveness and so to encourage students to work harder. But those clinging to the primacy of British practice sometimes see this as undermining standards and eroding subtle distinctions in performance. In fact, these practices usually just formalise what has been found to be the results over a number of years. They in no way indicate that the marking has necessarily become formulaic or unsubtle. Indeed, most of those who complain about the system admit that their marks were in practice largely as expected – and quite often better.

CATEGORIES OF ASSESSMENT

Many students comment on what they see as not only different but dubious methods of assessment in use abroad. When they are given marks for class attendance, for example, British students can feel as outraged as Cromwell was to discover that the primary qualification for voting in a democracy is the ability to breathe. Marks for participating in seminar discussions or for raising points in lectures are often seen as equally spurious, though none-the-less welcome when generously bestowed. Take-home exams, open-book, honour-bound, unsupervised tests, multiple choices, quizzes and group marking may all create similar concerns.

Yet none of these things is exactly unknown in Britain. In all cases, what you are encountering in assessment abroad, as in other aspects of teaching and learning, is a range which is different from, and sometimes more diverse than, that which you have met at home. That should not surprise and need not concern. There is sometimes a reluctance to concede that different methods have their merits. But they clearly do and their rationale, if not obvious immediately, may become clearer in time. Taken in the right spirit, any novelty can add something to your study repertoire.

SUMMARY

To cope with study and teaching methods abroad, you will need to:

- Be prepared for differences
- Be willing to relearn
- Be flexible
- Be adaptable
- Use a range of skills
- Resolve language issues
- Seek advice
- Try things first

SOME QUESTIONS

What can you discover in your own university about teaching and learning methods in its partner institutions? How much of an adjustment do you expect to have to make? Which forms of assessment suit you best? Where would you turn for guidance or advice on different study methods?

14 STUDYING IN A NEW ENVIRONMENT

'It's not just a year of study. Do as much as you can. You won't regret it.'

'It was an awesome experience – though I don't think that the actual programme was that. It was more just the period abroad that was so beneficial.'

Becoming an international student is more than simply adjusting to different learning and teaching styles. It is also coming to terms with a different environment, a new university and a new country. As is well known, the term 'university', despite strenuous efforts of late to limit its use and prevent its abuse, has never been narrowly defined. Each university is different, in size, in appearance, in character. Each country is, of course, unique. This chapter looks at some of the non-academic factors that can affect your study in a new environment, and considers some of the skills that you will have to deploy if you are to feel at home there.

RESOURCES

One of the learning elements on which students abroad most often comment is the provision of resources. Some universities are endowed like banks and often resemble them in the echoing vastness of their principal buildings. Others have infinitely more modest means and seem more like run-down hotels in unfashionable parts of towns. Though these elements are very striking and are usually what you notice first, afterwards they seem to make surprisingly little difference to the quality of the study experience.

For most of us, it is probably easier to adjust to glut than to famine, and those who find their host university offers more resources than they are used to will probably take to the new situation quite readily. But glut brings its own problems in requiring you to be more widely knowledgeable and discriminating. A very large campus which has to be mastered with the aid of a map, rather like a city, is going to be explored only gradually. Getting used to less, however, is not straightforward either. If you are not already familiar with them, rationed availability of books or timed computer access, for example, do require some alterations to your study methods. But most people learn to cope soon enough.

LIBRARIES

In Britain every student is introduced to the university library and is asked to treat it as a major study resource. But libraries, like universities, follow no blueprints. They vary greatly from institution to institution. They are arranged in different ways and they operate in different ways. Books are classified and stacked on different principles. Different practices also govern rules on borrowing. Institutions which have scarce library resources will be anxious to regulate and define access to their collection. Their procedures may be complex or unusual for you. All this, of course, needs your early and close attention. Wherever you are, you have to be able to find the books you need promptly.

You also have to know what other facilities the library can offer. Can you get access to on-line data within the library? Will the library be able to obtain material for you through inter-library loan? Are there catalogues available of what can be found in libraries nearby, which you can use? Are audio-visual materials, recorded television programmes, for example, available there? Can you obtain newspapers, including those from other countries, such as Britain? Mastering a new library can add immensely to your feeling of being in control of your studies. It is also important if you are to achieve your academic goals, particularly when you need to find alternatives to things you made much use of at home.

Books and borrowing

If, in the new library, shelving is a mystery and the catalogue an enigma, it can take time before you are using the place confidently. But, because you may well have to use many different libraries throughout your career, the struggle for mastery is definitely beneficial. Once more, what you encounter at first as an unwelcome problem will turn out in time to be a valuable extension to your knowledge in dealing with any new academic environment. As in other study matters, what you learn can be adapted to other situations. You will enhance your skills. Most libraries supply guides. If you arm yourself with those and begin just by wandering around the open stacks, finding out what is in the closed ones, using the catalogue and then getting access to the books, your grasp of what is involved will soon become more assured.

In some universities abroad, you may find that students use the library less than in Britain and sometimes rely instead on buying textbooks. In other cases, borrowing is required but restricted and you have to read the books in the library building. Some libraries make extracts of key texts available for you to examine individually, sometimes photocopied or on computer. The intention is to ensure that everyone has access to a particular body of literature, regarded as fundamental for the course, at all times. The drawback, perhaps, is that you are obliged to spend more time reading in the library. In other cases, libraries will offer you extensive borrowing rights. Some provide multiple copies of books in demand; others expect you to be able to cope with a single copy which is made available to each reader for a short period at a time, perhaps only for a few hours. In other words, depending on what you find, you may have to adjust your usual work patterns so as to be able to study in different places, to cope with scarce (or plentiful) resources, and to match your learning style to the constraints on the availability of materials. These are all study skills, too. They will take time to master but will prove useful once you've done so.

COMPUTERS

Some universities employ computers to a far greater (and others to a far smaller) degree than you may be familiar with in Britain. If you are required to produce all your written work and to conduct all your communication with staff on-line, your skills in this area will be at a premium. You may feel at a stretch, unless you have sufficient experience and are familiar with what is involved. By contrast, if computer use is very much more restricted than in Britain, you may find you have to revert to the use of a typewriter or to hand-written script, which can be surprisingly difficult. But that is distinctly unusual: most universities can now offer students some access to computers.

If computers are in widespread use, there will also be a specialist service for students who require assistance, as you will have at home. That's where you should look for advice on honing your skills. Almost every university expects to initiate new students into its ways and, today, computer literacy is certainly one of the skills that nearly all academic institutions hope to teach. Most will offer training courses on the preferred local styles or personal back-up or assistance, if you feel that is all you need. Working without some computer aid which you employ at home is usually more difficult than learning new programmes but there is a gain in each because each requires you to explore alternative methods of coping.

LIFELONG LEARNING COURSES

Some universities provide courses not only in academic subjects but in various vocational and recreational subjects of interest to students. In the Britain, these are normally provided externally by the Continuing Education or Lifelong Learning division of the institution and it is sometimes a shock to British students to discover them on offer abroad to full-time undergraduates. Some students even regard it as an indication that standards have collapsed and that 'Mickey Mouse' disciplines are invading the curriculum. The concern is almost certainly misplaced. These courses don't substitute for academic courses but supplement them. They relate to a much older idea, once popular in British universities, too, and still found in schools, of education as catering to the 'whole person'. They are meant to indicate that study needs to be rooted in daily life rather than abstracted from it.

If you are confronted with courses in traditional dance or in table tennis or some other unlikely field, there is no reason why you should not think of tackling them in that same spirit. This means, among other things, recognising them as supplementary and not expecting that they will count towards your transferred credit. The hope is that these courses will engage your interest, improve your skills in socially useful and responsible ways, and provide you with like-minded company and a relaxing break from more demanding studies.

COPING WITH DISTRACTIONS

Many study guides emphasise how important it is for a successful student to have a home environment that is supportive of your studies. If those around you resent the fact that you are studying and often try to distract you, it can undermine your best efforts. Being abroad may bring new problems in this respect. You are a lot further from the work routines and disciplines learned at home. The distractions are also likely to be more numerous. Your fellow students and flat-mates may include some who are not studying for credit and who may be determined not to take their studies too seriously. Being abroad means that you are more on your own in coping with such problems. You won't necessarily have the evident support of your institution or your fellow students. This may require you to set limits on how much distraction you will allow. Again the experience, however trying, will be to your advantage later.

Study guides usually recommend that you try to negotiate terms. A compromise is often possible. You can agree to devote time to doing the things your colleagues want to do, on condition that they then allow you time to study. The problem is that the time you need to study is specific to you and sometimes to the project you are undertaking and may not be easily negotiable on some routine basis. Where compromise fails, you may either have to confront and challenge those who are distracting you or you may have to change where and when you work to find the conditions that suit you.

SOCIAL LIFE

Finding a balance between work and study is just as important abroad as it is at home. Students sometimes remark that it can be disappointing when some of the social supports on which they rely at home are missing. Many students miss particularly the societies and clubs that feature prominently in British academic life but which are not always as much in evidence elsewhere. The disappointment is particularly keen if local students traditionally desert the campus in the evening or go home at the weekends, as is not unusual in some places. It can be equally disorienting when local students form exclusive associations to which others have limited access. Fraternities and sororities in North America or 'nations' in Europe can seem oddly alienating even when they are, in fact, prepared to admit others.

Building a social life for yourself abroad is another life skill which is often honed abroad. If you are denied on-campus companionship, you have a motive to go exploring and to find company in other ways. Almost everyone in a new academic environment feels socially isolated to a degree at first. You have left your family and friends behind you and you hope to replace them with new friends, which is unlikely to happen overnight. There is no formula for making friends anywhere. But everyone is agreed that, when you do make the effort, ultimately it will almost always be rewarded.

EXPLORING

The search for friends is one aspect of a prime goal for Study Abroad students – getting to know a new country. Though study is important, so, too, is taking advantage of your time abroad to learn something at first hand about the people and country you are visiting. Those who fail to explore this side of their stay invariably feel disappointed and deprived. Some students argue, admittedly with suspicious enthusiasm sometimes, that you learn more as you move around and observe your new environment than you could possibly do in any classroom. But there is some truth in it. Even when the host university or college does not meet your highest social expectations, the experience of building acquaintances in a new country can more than make up for this.

Perhaps the reason for this is obvious. Virtually all you gain from studying abroad could be achieved were you to encounter the teachers and fellow students at home, which is perfectly possible. What is unique is the experience of coping with a wholly new environment. Coping generally lies in the area of life skills rather than purely academic skills; but the two cannot, of course, be separated. The confidence you gain from being able to deal with the situations you encounter abroad extends to everything you do, the academic and non-academic alike.

TRAVEL AND CULTURAL OPPORTUNITIES

Most countries offer special travel opportunities for students in term time and in vacations. Often fares on planes, boats or trains are discounted. To benefit from these, you generally need no special requirements, except some proof of your student status. You should certainly take an early opportunity to enquire locally. In some cases, it is useful to buy an International Student Travel Card because this can be used in making purchases and as a form of identity in asking for concessionary entry into museums or galleries or sites of historical interest. There are also sometimes special student days or periods in museums and galleries when entry is provided free. You need to know about them if you are to turn up at the right time. Local tourist information offices should be able to provide details.

When you have the chance to travel, you may also find hostels and small hotels which cater specially for you. These places are generally basic to the point of being Spartan, but they are always good value and are often helpful for meeting other students and finding information on what there is to do locally. These days, there are also internet cafés where you can gain e-mail access (at a small cost) and so be able to keep in touch with everyone: your family, friends, and home and host universities. You may also find student deals in restaurants or shops which can help to conserve your budget if you know where to look. Your host university's student organisation is usually the best place to enquire initially.

ACADEMIC TOURISM

It is wrong to regard all this as just a fringe benefit. In recent years some travel companies have begun to offer what they call 'academic tourism', trips abroad which have the further purpose of allowing the participants to gain some knowledge of the place visited (its language, history, architecture or whatever). Study Abroad students are not academic tourists. You generally stay much longer, which is an indication of what you can hope to achieve. You also study more intensively and usually with a sharper focus. Your main interest is in your discipline, not just in local colour. Above all, you are there not just to observe but to become part of the local academic community.

This aim of belonging as students within a society, however temporarily, makes for a real difference. The ultimate goal is not to remain in a foreign cocoon while learning about and witnessing local life from afar. It is to be absorbed. In their academic work, Study Abroad students have to conform to the requirements of the courses they attend. They generally have to follow local students with regard to what they can study and often how they study it. The approaches they take to understanding their subjects are those that are recommended locally. And their work is assessed by criteria determined for local students. In the same way, by living and travelling locally, you have an opportunity not just to learn about, but to experience, local life. The difference may be subtle at times, but it is certainly there.

OBSERVATION AND PERCEPTION

In the book trade, there is a recognised category called travel literature. It includes guidebooks and lavishly illustrated coffee-table books, but its staple is the work which tries to capture something not only of a particular setting but also of the people who live there at a moment in history. Jan Morris, one of the most distinguished practitioners of the genre, sees her work as illustrating 'the shifting responses of a single mind, faced with the slow unfolding of the planet'. The skills which this involves – observation, interpretation, categorisation – are very relevant, too, to the experience of the student on Study Abroad.

Study Abroad students also have the chance to apply their minds to the passing scene and to observe the evolution of the society in which they have come to live. Not to do so would be to miss half the benefit and more than half of the pleasure. You are not required to produce a work of literature from your observations nor even to write down your thoughts at all. But it is expected that you will make use of your situation to enhance your own understanding of the world about you. You, too, need to be open to experience, to search for understanding and to try to assess what you witness. Students often testify to the pleasure and sense of achievement this brings. Nearly everyone feels not only that they have begun to come to terms with another society but also that they have, as a result, been forced to reflect more deeply on their own. Quite a large number judge this to be the most valuable lesson of all.

SUMMARY

Adaptation requires you to respond to:

- The size of the institution and its facilities
- Local library and computer resources
- Vocational and recreational courses
- Study distractions and social isolation
- Opportunities for observation

SOME QUESTIONS

Where do you study normally and where would you most prefer? What facilities do you think you require to ensure that you work successfully? In what way in the past has being in a new environment contributed to your understanding as a student?

15 INTERCULTURAL COMMUNICATION

'It can be frustrating when you are in a new culture and have to adjust to it quickly. But it gets easier and it gets more and more enjoyable. Don't be misled by stereotypes about surly foreigners. People will happily talk to you if you are ready to approach them. You just have to take the initiative and to be brave.'

'Open your mind. Do not cling to fellow Brits. It seems hard and you may resent the new culture at first because you don't understand it. But when the time comes to go home, you'll realise that you love the place and will want to get back a.s.a.p.'

Central to study abroad is a desire to communicate within another culture. All Study Abroad students have to grapple with this whether they intend to or not. Intercultural communication, as it is called, is now a major subject of scholarly research, and a great deal has been published about it. But, despite this, communicating across cultures is still a big challenge. It is far more than simply mastering a different language, just as sharing a language is not in itself evidence of sharing a culture. It is also more than observing culture difference though that is often the first step. This chapter considers some of the issues which Study Abroad students in particular are likely to confront.

CULTURE AND UNDERSTANDING

Those who have studied abroad usually claim that one of the main benefits is to learn how to communicate better with the local population. They regard this as central to getting to know another country and to feeling at home there. Intercultural communication, they suggest, has two aspects. On the one hand, studying abroad makes it necessary for you to be able to deal with at least the most obvious aspects of the local culture in order to be comfortable and relaxed. On the other hand, you are likely to find yourself regarded by the locals, at least in part, as an outsider, which forces you to think more about who you are and what your purpose is in being there. It isn't always very comfortable being an outsider, observing rather than belonging, even though it could be claimed that that posture is, to an extent, characteristic of the scholar everywhere. Some of the insights you acquire are no doubt bought by hard-won experience which may be why they then seem so valuable.

The opportunities for gaining intercultural skills are certainly among the richest experiences that Study Abroad offers. They are also among the more testing. Almost everyone involved in the process senses that they have embarked on a voyage of discovery. Most ultimately judge that the journey has enriched them but many testify to the tensions they experienced along the way. An outsider is an object of interest and curiosity to some locals, of indifference and suspicion (even of resentment and distrust) to others. You may begin by deciding that to live comfortably in a new community you will want to feel worthy of the interest or be able to overcome the suspicion. But it is not always a straightforward matter.

SUBMERGED CULTURE

Some writers suggest that a culture is like an iceberg. There is a part you can observe and can cope with quite readily, such as differences in language or dress, and there is a much larger submerged part, such as belief systems or customs, which you cannot see and against which it is rather easy to offend. When you are trying to communicate, it is usually the submerged part of the culture that forms the unforeseen obstacle. It makes it no easier that submerged differences are often encountered in areas where we are all peculiarly sensitive, in gender relations, in rules on politeness, in our sense of humour or in our attitude to loss.

Becoming aware of an unconscious or hidden element in cultural interaction is disorienting at first and can then bring a real sense of discovery. On finding that cultures diverge as well as converge, you are likely to respond initially by feeling puzzled or even hurt. The worst thing is that you seem to have lost your instinctive sense of what is 'natural'. For a time, you may even feel cut off from safe cultural moorings. Ultimately, however, your discovery is enlightening, perhaps transforming. You realise that cultural divergence is something that everyone encounters who lives abroad, and it is possible to be alert to it and even to find the subject fascinating.

DENYING DIFFERENCES

Study Abroad, which generally involves a short but intense exposure to a different culture, can often involve situations in which issues of cultural communication arise. Few people are prepared for this. Most of us – particularly when we are travelling abroad – like to feel that we are citizens of the world. We tend to stress our international awareness and to emphasise how alike all peoples are in the end. We often laugh at 'national characteristics' and are critical of those who claim to detect ethnic or racial differences between peoples. We try to blend in, drink the local brew and insist that globalisation is eroding all differences in culture. This is not mere self-delusion. Finding our common humanity is crucial to all forms of cultural communication.

But it is also true that different communities do manifest cultural differences and that these differences can render communication between one community and another complex and subtle. It helps to be sensitive to this. When communicating with others across cultures, you may experience reactions which seem unexpected or mysterious at first. These are not things which you should ignore or allow simply to irritate you. They are worth reflecting on and exploring. You have to be aware that you are, and that others will take you to be, a representative of your culture. Despite your best intentions, you will confirm this in many of the things you do and say. When you find yourself puzzled, it is likely that your reaction was provoked either by you failing to be aware of some cultural sensitivity on the part of your listeners or by them failing to be aware of some cultural sensitivity on your part.

GOING NATIVE

In the days when Britain had an empire, the idea of 'going native' was one of the more cardinal sins. You were expected to maintain your national identity, appearance and values at all costs. Today, for many people, almost the opposite is true. You want to be thought completely at home in every society you visit and preferably invisible within it. In other words, most people want to feel completely accepted as someone with an instinctive understanding of local ways and able to share in every way in the life of the community. Many of us often regard people who insist on maintaining their own culture abroad – 'full English breakfasts on the Riviera', for example – as reverting to imperial ways. In our eyes, they can often be wilfully giving offence. To find that we ourselves are capable of seeming foreign is not at all comfortable.

On the other hand, your hosts may see you as interesting precisely because you don't entirely share their culture. While, no doubt, they welcome your interest in them, they may even be offended if you claim identity with them or imitate their dress or use some of their characteristic phrases. Imitation is said to be the sincerest form of flattery. But it is sometimes done to denigrate or deride. Going native may require some prior evidence of cultural sympathy. Your hosts will probably be certain in their minds that you don't share their culture, however much you imitate it. Indeed, it may give them confidence that you, as a stranger, are in this respect inevitably in need of their advice. After all, you cannot be as familiar with that culture as someone who has been part of it since birth.

CULTURE AND SYMPATHY

Study Abroad allows you rare opportunities to explore these issues and to learn how to build cultural connections. You not only work alongside people from another country, you enjoy opportunities for relaxation and recreation with them as well. To benefit from the experience to the fullest extent, all aspects of life need to be considered significant. Because so much of culture (yours as well as theirs) is hidden and unconscious, you may first need to be on the lookout. Quite often, awareness is achieved almost accidentally, provided you have become sensitive to it. Many students say that they found they made progress once they put their expectations aside and tried consciously to observe and not to judge. That allowed them to begin to understand the society in which they had come to live on its own terms.

On returning from India, which they had come to admire tremendously, Lytton Strachey's eccentric family set all their clocks to Indian time and insisted on sleeping when everyone else at home was working and getting up when everyone else was going to bed. That today might be regarded as a genuine but overenthusiastic response to the challenge of cultural communication. A more contemporary approach would require you to try to respect both cultures equally and to adapt to whatever time is in use locally. To gain a sympathetic understanding of your hosts' culture does not require you to follow it slavishly. It does require you to show a great deal of respectful interest. You certainly need to be observant, inquisitive about social sensitivities and conscious of where obstacles to communication might lie. And this also has to be done cautiously, discreetly and politely. If you are always assuming difference (particularly where none exists), you will give the impression of being unhappy in your host society and homesick.

STEREOTYPES

One of the main reasons for difficulties in cultural communication is stereotyping. In an age when racist behaviour is a crime and when being enlightened means being free from prejudice, it is hard to recognise that we are all inclined to see the world in stereotypes. But only a few moments of introspection indicate that we do. When we use terms like 'the French' or 'Africans', we may be aware that they are so broad that it is impossible to generalise from them. But we do generalise from them, sometimes frequently, and we do invest our generalisations with meaning. On some occasions, the generalisation may be flattering. Mostly it is not. On all occasions, what is argued will, at best, be true of part of the group but not true of all. Stereotypes seem to be used because they allow us to make sense of an impossibly complex world. But they do undoubtedly influence the way in which we regard one another. Even if we feel we can put them aside in face-to-face contact with individuals, they affect us in other contexts and in other ways.

Many international students argue that they have been the victims of stereotyping. Students from Britain are often aware of being seen as class conscious or stand-offish or prudish or insular or imperialistic or chauvinistic. Sometimes they are also seen as intensely democratic, orderly, tolerant and polite, which is generally more encouraging. But it would be easy to pick out British people who are none of those things. We less often appreciate that we make similarly wild assumptions about others. Encountering soft-spoken and self-effacing Americans and amusing and witty Germans is really not difficult. Study Abroad can provide an opportunity for you to look at your own stereotypes and to test them against reality. It can be a devastating experience. Such comforting cultural myths are not always easy to dislodge.

TALKING POLITICS

As an instance of difficulty in cultural communication, students often remark on how challenging it is to discuss your own nation's political standpoints with students in another country. Whereas at home we may regard ourselves as critics of the government and satirists of national social attitudes, abroad many of us immediately leap to their defence. Perhaps we are simply anxious to counter the stereotyping which we feel enters into anyone else's comments on our nation's politics. Perhaps we suspect that respect for us as individuals must begin with respect for our country. Something at any rate causes us often to exaggerate our national loyalty and to suppress our sympathy with those whom we probably suspect are not fully informed critics.

In general, disagreement is not usually a problem for students. Everyone recognises that criticism is healthy and that to explore with others their political opinions can be genuinely revealing and helpful. But, particularly on issues where there is very largely a consensus at home with which we tend to agree (on issues such as capital punishment, for example), it is disturbing to find that very different opinions can prevail about them elsewhere. Suddenly, from being in a large and contented majority, you may find yourself in a beleaguered, embattled minority. This is a real opportunity to discover the strength of the home consensus but it is hard initially to see it like that. Yet it is only by being challenged but not being provoked (and not feeling threatened) that you may ultimately break through to a deeper understanding of the contrary opinions you hear. Whether you succeed or not seems sometimes to depend on how far you have been able to break through socially and to gain a respect for those who have voiced the contrary opinion.

DRINK, DRUGS AND SEX

Cultural issues extend into the whole area of lifestyle, and occasionally students feel concerned in encountering a social practice abroad which they find gives concern or offence. This can involve matters of health or good taste where we are least inclined to be relativist. In general, you can respond by trying to ignore it or by talking it over with others. By the time you are studying abroad, you have probably become well used to other students whose tastes differ from your own or whose lifestyle or conduct seems to you unwise. You have probably learned how to avoid taking – or giving – offence. You will be conscious that individuals are entitled to live their lives as they choose, so long as this is within the law. You will also know that, even where social pressure to conform is often heavy, there are ways and means of coping with it if you would rather not follow suit. The situation abroad is not fundamentally different.

It is true, of course, that the law is not the same in all countries, particularly for those of student age. Custom, too, may differ. Only a generation ago, British students attending social events in American universities were shocked at the amount of alcohol consumed. Since then, the law has altered and it is now more likely to be the American students in Britain who voice the complaint. There are often differences between countries in the tolerance of drug use and in laws governing sexual or gender relations. Even when the law is silent, there may be local university regulations or popular customs on what is permissible and not permissible, as on matters concerning sexual harassment, for example. You clearly need to be aware of local attitudes and sensitive to what is judged appropriate if you are to avoid giving offence.

NAMES AND TITLES

One aspect of adapting to another culture that often creates difficulty is the use of different forms of names and titles. At first, you may find local names rather strange and difficult to remember and may feel unsure of the form of address considered most appropriate in talking to locals. Many societies have conventions about this which differ strikingly from the custom in Britain. Some of these rules are hugely complex and subtle and involve different forms of address between different social groups. The United Kingdom has a reputation for academic informality (though this does not necessarily apply to everyone in every institution). But it is always best abroad to begin by assuming that formality is to be preferred to informality unless you are specifically told otherwise.

If it is important to you that people are polite and courteous and that they do not assume too great an intimacy or too much formality in the way they deal with you, then you ought to recognise that locals will feel the same about themselves. They won't expect you to get forms of address right immediately because they will know that other outsiders also have problems with this. But they will hope that you care enough about them to want to try. If they tell you how to address them, you can adopt this and ignore anything else. Otherwise you should strive to follow polite, respectful local usage.

Academic address

Academics should always be addressed at first by their title or honorific, as you might use 'Doctor' or 'Professor' in Britain. Even if you find the titles complicated and difficult, you should not simply give up and brazen things out on the grounds that a foreigner cannot be expected to understand them. If you want to give the impression of being respectful, you have to anticipate that practice may differ from home. This doesn't require you to get everything right. If initially you make a mistake, it is enough to indicate, when corrected, that you recognise the error.

In time, as in Britain, many university teachers may ask you to use more familiar forms of address which is usually quite straightforward to do. A few students are uncomfortable with informality in an academic context. If so, no one is going to be offended by your continuing to prefer the polite form. As in other areas, the best policy is to watch what your fellow students do and then model yourself on them. When they seem to regard formality or informality as normal, perhaps it will feel more appropriate for you to do so, too. Between one another, most students everywhere usually prefer friendliness and openness to correctness. Making the effort to communicate is regarded as much more important than following every local convention. But it is wise to be cautious.

HOMESICKNESS

Issues in cultural communication are often behind an attack of homesickness. Homesickness is experienced by many students who study abroad though it is seldom very severe. It is usually at its worst a few weeks after first arrival. Once the initial excitement wears off, you sometimes encounter with full force the problems of dealing with a new environment. You may find yourself in an unfamiliar place in which such apparently simple matters as posting a letter or taking a bus have become unexpectedly complicated. Such problems are not really complex but, coming one on top of the other at a time when you are missing home comforts or home company, they can get past your defences. You have to tell yourself that this is all part of the experience, that others have also gone through it, and that, by overcoming it, you will ultimately emerge as a stronger, more resilient, more confident person. It helps enormously if you can see the funny side of your misunderstandings, too.

On a few occasions the problem persists. The ease with which home can be contacted nowadays, by phone, fax or e-mail, the sheer speed of modern communications, sometimes make it more difficult to break away. You can neglect the effort to come to terms with your host society and remain in, but largely separate from, your new environment. Some people also find that solving the simpler problems of culture contact seems only to introduce them to larger and more intractable ones. When you have settled down and are working hard and then find that making friends locally is difficult, for example, the effect is likely to be to add to any feelings of homesickness. If the feeling is persistent and troubling, it is important to seek help. You need to feel reasonably relaxed and confident in order to work well. Feeling confused, unhappy and ill at ease is going to have the opposite effect. There are usually fellow students, tutors and even professional advisers to whom you can turn. But this is a matter which seems to take its own time to resolve.

Home from home

The ability to be at ease socially with people from other cultures is no doubt the product of many things, not least background and personality. It is also a matter of the skills that everyone learns over time. Some of the required skills are linguistic, and practice and experience with local usage help enormously here. Some of them are behavioural, which can be harder. Body language, for example, is not always easy to interpret or translate, far less to follow. Sometimes what is most required to bridge any cultural divide is greater understanding, deriving from knowledge, study and observation. Sometimes it is a shift in attitude which can take place only if your feelings are engaged.

It is scarcely surprising if not all students get far down the road to biculturalism or multiculturalism – or even want to. Yet, in the time allowed, nearly everyone shows evidence of making some progress in this respect. Only a few will have the opportunity or the inclination to do more. There are particular disincentives for the anglophone when most of the world now has some knowledge of English and of British (or more often American) culture. But getting by is not getting on. Even if the road is a long one, everyone will tell you that it is the journey, not the arrival, that matters.

SUMMARY

In learning about another culture, you should be prepared:

- To be regarded as an outsider
- To learn about yourself

- To discover submerged cultural differences
- To feel defensively patriotic
- To find ambiguity in integration
- To respect cultural pluralism
- To cope with homesickness
- To live with stereotyping
- To be tolerant of difference
- To observe formalities

SOME QUESTIONS

Do you think language is a bigger barrier to communication between cultures than custom or belief? What stereotypes have you encountered about your own country and how valid are they in your view? What is your cure for homesickness?

16 RE-ENTRY

'This was a great experience. My confidence is higher. I know I have lived abroad and coped with all the difficulties this posed.'

'A year ago I did not look forward to leaving home. Now I don't want to go back.'

The final stage in Study Abroad, departure and arrival back home, is often the least considered. Problems of re-entry, however, can be as real for international students as they are for astronauts. This chapter looks at some of the major issues involved and considers how these might be tackled before you leave and after you've returned.

TRANSCRIPTS

Having studied abroad, you will want to know before you return home, that all is in place to ensure that your academic record will be made available to your home university. That is why you went, after all. Normally, the host university will produce a transcript for you. This will include an account of all the courses you have taken and the grades you have obtained. If it is not in a standard and agreed format, like that for ECTS, some supplementary comments on your performance may be included and some guidelines provided for those who will have to translate the transcript's terms into the terms employed in your home university. If the transcript is not in English, you may have to obtain a translation, though that is a matter for your home university to decide. You should have no problem, provided the language in use is a familiar one, but it is worth checking.

You also need to ensure before leaving that the transcript is being prepared and that you have provided any information which is required. You ought to find out how the transcript will be sent. Will it come directly to you for onward transmission or will it go to the Study Abroad office in your university or to a named individual or to your department or school? If your study was part of an exchange, it is unlikely that the transcript will come directly to you. But that does not exempt you entirely from responsibility for its production. You must be certain that your host university has a reliable forwarding address for any correspondence that will come to you directly.

Delays

Transcripts can take some time to be completed and to arrive. If some of your assessed work was not submitted until near the end of your time abroad, it can take some weeks before the assessment is done and the grades returned to the central records agency. The markers or recorders may not show the same degree of urgency that you feel about this, particularly if they are about to embark on the start of their annual leave. Because your position is unusual (the other students in your classes will presumably be continuing with their studies), it may not be fully realised that you need this to be done. To encourage everyone to produce the transcript promptly and accurately, you have obligations to get your work done on time and to check that everything has been received.

You ought also to make clear any deadlines involved. Some students need to have their studies abroad recognised in order to proceed into the next stage of their course or to be allowed to attend the next graduation. Failure to produce the transcript on time could, if things go drastically wrong, mean delays or even force you into repeating parts of the study. If you have deadlines, it makes sense to tell your host university what those are and why they are there. You can then hope to have their co-operation in ensuring that the deadlines are met.

SETTLING AFFAIRS

On a very few occasions, your departure from your host university will be noted for all the wrong reasons. It is most important that you check what obligations you are required to fulfil in giving up your accommodation, terminating your membership of any organisations (like sports groups or student unions), surrendering your library card and handing in your keys to more-or-less anything. If you haven't paid a phone bill, an electricity bill or a book fine, irate international letters will fly between your host and your home universities for months to come, with unfortunate effects on an institutional goodwill that has probably been built up over many years. Many UK universities respond to such crises by issuing you with the threat that you will not be allowed to graduate until the outstanding amount is settled. The need for everyone to honour their obligations to their partners is taken very seriously.

If you have inadvertently forgotten something which will cause your hosts embarrassment, try to get in touch immediately with some appropriate person and confess. Once it is known that you are accepting responsibility, the anger immediately vanishes from the correspondence. Anyone can make a mistake. What causes the concern is the suspicion that you might have vanished in the night in the belief that you are unlikely to be traceable across frontiers. That impression will be doubly strong if your forgetfulness relates not to the host university itself but to some members of the wider public whom it has contracted to look after you, such as a home-stay or hospitality family.

RE-ORIENTATION

Many students end their period abroad by getting a vacation job or taking a break before returning home. There is often no better way of consolidating your sense of being at ease outside your own country. You can rub shoulders with a wider cross-section of society than a university offers and deepen your understanding of the local culture, while also setting yourself up financially or recharging your emotional batteries for the period ahead. Many people find this a helpful change of gear, moving on from one set of experiences abroad to another before returning to the fray at home.

What you must remember to do is to keep in touch during this interval. The host university may be anxious to establish contact to discuss not just things you have overlooked but matters relating to your course on which they will have to report. If you are in limbo for three months, it causes serious delays. Your home university may be even more anxious to get in touch about the following year when matters have to be arranged or altered. The local education authority, responsible for arranging your fee payments, may have some questions. If you can provide a contact address (perhaps someone you will ring or e-mail periodically and who would be willing to forward messages for you) it avoids the delays and ensures that you can deal with anything that cannot wait until your return.

TIME AND CHANGE

The major adjustment which faces you begins once you get back home. Returning from Study Abroad, many students are surprised to be told they have changed, though they are often aware that they now see their life at home differently. The most obvious reason for the comment is that the experience of studying overseas is dramatic compared to remaining in Britain. One consequence is that returnees are all too inclined to talk about their experience to anyone who will listen. Even the most loyal of friends complain when you are forever comparing things at home with those you have known abroad (and usually unfavourably). There are deeper issues, too. It is very unlikely that you will be – or will seem to be – in your views or your demeanour precisely the same as the person who left. You have been forced into a greater degree of independence abroad, into more self-reliance and more self-questioning. This is likely to communicate itself to your family, your friends and to the academic staff. Because they have not had time to adjust to the changes, as those with you abroad will have done, you may find the restoration of customary social relations takes more effort than you might have supposed.

The other revelation is that everyone else has changed, too, even though less markedly perhaps than you have. Time has passed, water has flowed under the bridge and things are not exactly as you remember them. In your absence, all sorts of events will have taken place to which you must now adjust. Much will depend, of course, on how far you have travelled and how long the interval between your departure and return. But it is unlikely that you will be able to take up exactly where you left off, unless you have particularly complacent relatives and friends.

ASSESSING THE EXPERIENCE

It is useful to begin quite soon to set your overseas experience into a context for yourself. Many exchange universities will ask you to complete a questionnaire for them and perhaps your own university will do so, too. They will want to know how you viewed the experience. What were the strengths and what were the weaknesses? How useful was the guidance provided at each stage? What would you have liked to have done differently? Do you see ways of improving the experience for those who will come after you? If you are not required to answer such questions, you should consider doing so for yourself and then sending your report to your Study Abroad office or your academic adviser. This exercise is what civil servants call a debriefing and it is an enormously helpful way of realising what you have achieved and allowing others to appreciate what they might find in the future.

Your home university has a major interest in your impressions. It has approved the programme on which you have been sent. It now needs to know from you how successful this has been and what can be done to improve it. Your views will be used when the Study Abroad arrangements are renegotiated, and you should be frank if you feel there is anything amiss. What you write may also serve as the basis of the instructions which will be prepared for students applying for the following year. This will help them make up their minds about what to do and what to avoid. You may also be invited to talk directly to students about your experiences. Study Abroad staff may interview you, particularly if your comments have raised further questions for them. Finally, what you have to say will also interest the Quality Assessment inspectors when, in time, they visit your university to assess its courses.

RE-ESTABLISHING CONTACT

Once you return, you should think of letting your academic adviser abroad know that you have got back safely. This is a courtesy and one that will be appreciated. But it is also a means of reminding everyone that you are no longer a student there and that the necessary processes need to be undertaken to ensure that the exchange arrangements are completed. It is, in addition, a means of keeping open the communication so that, if you need their support or advice in future, you have already prepared the way. It is even more of a courtesy if you can say how much you have enjoyed your time abroad and the opportunity to be a student there (assuming, of course, that you have and that you are not about to sue them).

Some overseas universities will want you to register with their alumni organisations, which is another useful way of keeping in touch. Students sometimes return to the university they have visited to undertake part of their postgraduate work or even to complete a further degree. Keeping in touch ensures that you have a contact point, if and when you decide to go back. You may also need references from your time abroad (they tend to impress employers). This could be a good time to write to ask for permission to use the names of those you think have formed a good opinion of your work (though it may be even better to do this, face to face, before you leave). At any rate, a note reporting on your safe arrival home is a means of ensuring that you are kept in mind a little longer even if, alas, you cannot always expect the memory to be retained irrevocably.

REMEMBERING FRIENDS

You probably need no urging to keep in touch with your newly made friends. That is a pleasure, not an obligation. You may already have made arrangements to meet in the future, on a home or away basis. But it is not always realised how quickly and how easily you can lose touch with them once you are back on course at home. In terms of mastering intercultural skills, they are not incidental to your achievements. Their friendship is an important part of what you have gained by studying abroad. If you value that friendship, you may have to make an effort to keep it alive.

Keeping in touch has never been easier. When you travel, there is no way to avoid distances or time differences but, seated at your desk, you can establish electronic or telephonic contact in an instant. That is not to say that your message will be received instantly or will be responded to immediately – you are not the only person who goes travelling – but it will certainly be welcomed provided you haven't inadvertently called in the middle of the night. To arrange reunions does require rather more thought and effort. But there are ways and means, and you will have gained a new interest in any opportunities which arise.

LOOKING AHEAD

Arranging to return to your studies at home may seem as easy as falling off a log – and just as unwelcome. But you can avoid any sense of let-down by giving the matter some thought. One way of building up an excitement at the prospect of returning is to find out what has been happening in your absence. It is quite likely that changes will have been made at your institution of which you are unaware and about which no one will have thought of telling you. A popular solution is to hunt down some old classmates and get them to spill the beans. This is, admittedly, surprisingly testing as it requires you not to spend the entire time talking about your own experiences.

It is to be hoped that everything you really need to have done to prepare for your future studies – making course choices and completing forms for fee support or accommodation or grants – will have been sent to you abroad. But there is an opportunity on your return to check and to plan ahead. Office staff are much more inclined to favour conversation in the vacation (except perhaps late on Fridays) and an early visit to your school or department to 'report back' could prove productive. Have a few questions ready to help things along. If you are passing on greetings messages from staff abroad, it may also be worth delivering them now. Greetings are likely to be received with greater enthusiasm before the pressures of term overwhelm their recipients. With a little luck, the goodwill which the message generates will envelop the messenger and you will feel welcomed back with acclaim.

SUMMARY

To prepare for re-entry, you need to:

- Make sure your transcript is prepared
- Leave a forwarding address and a contact address
- Explain any deadlines
- Ensure debts are paid and keys returned
- Be prepared for changes at home
- Do a debriefing
- Re-establish contacts abroad
- Report back

SOME QUESTIONS

What changes do you anticipate that a year will make to your institution? In what ways will a year abroad add to the interest of returning to your future studies at home? What opportunities do you have for feeding back your experiences within your institution?

A NOTE ON WEBSITES AND SOURCES

In recent years there has been a huge outpouring of books, articles and reports on internatioal student mobility. The Australian Council for Educational Research maintains a database on the subject which lists between fifty and a hundred pieces each month, principally works in English and chiefly from Australia and Britain. The website is at: http://cunningham.acer.edu.au/. If we were to compile a full world listing, it would surely run into thousands of items. Yet curiously little of this is of immediate relevance to students participating in the process, least of all to Study Abroad students. It is aimed mainly at the staff of institutions that participate in international education, particularly those that have developed a strong commercial interest in the subject.

In the United Kingdom, the most recent work in the field to attract attention has been the report on 'International Student Mobility', published in Bristol in July 2004 by the Higher Education Funding Council for England. The whole text is available on-line at http://www.hefce.ac.uk/pubs/hefce/2004/04_30/. Though not aimed primarily at students, it can be used as an introduction to the subject. It contains a helpful bibliography and has an index of the main bodies with an interest in international student mobility in Britain.

Many students begin their search for information outside their own university with the British Council. The Council has offices in virtually all the countries to which students have access, and most of these offices maintain individual websites with information relevant to those searching for Study Abroad opportunities. It is best approached through www.britishcouncil.org/home.htm.

For the European Union, there is a useful book, *Experience Erasmus – The UK Guide* (which will be in your university library) which lists all courses that make provision for a period of Erasmus study. There is also a vast number of websites on European exchanges. The most immediately useful is that of the UK Socrates/Erasmus Council: www.erasmus.ac.uk. It also offers links to other principal sources: www.erasmus.ac.uk/links.html. The Erasmus Student Committee is accessible at www.experience.erasmus.ac.uk. For the Bologna process, try www.europeunit.ac.uk. The main EU guide to the whole programme is at: http://europa.eu.int/comm/education/index_en.html. For Switzerland, which shadows Erasmus, you will need: http://www.crus.ch/engl/. A recent venture to supply more general, helpful information for students visiting Europe can be found at: http://europa.eu.int/ploteus/portal/home.jsp. With Ploteus we are back in Ancient Greece – it means 'navigator'.

The United States is even richer in information provision. As mentioned in the text, the best place to start is with the Bureau of Educational and Cultural Affairs of the US State Department. It maintains an excellent website at: http://educationusa.state.gov from which all sorts of information flows. It also publishes a little booklet, *If You Want to Study in the United States*, which is available in several subfields, including *Short-Term Study*. This can also be obtained at the same website. For exchanges, see http://www.exchanges.state.gov. The three sites mentioned in the text, IIE (http://www.iie.org), NAFSA (http://www.nafsa.org) and CIEE (http://www.ciee.org) are useful supplements. The IIE annual publication, *Open Doors*, gives the fullest statistical information on US international student mobility, both inwards and outwards. Useful for more general information about the US educational system are http://princetonreview.com and http://www.studyusa.com. For those hooked on league tables, there is endless delight available at: http://www.usnews.com/usnews/edu/college/rankings/rankindex_brief.php.

Australia is also well documented. You can choose between the approach of the university providers, IDP, at http://www.idp.edu.au/ or the government approach at http://aei.dest.gov.au/. For New Zealand, there is http://www.educationnz.org.nz and www.mynzed.com. For Canada, you can use the Canadian Bureau for International Education at: http://www.cbie.ca/ and www.cecnetwork.ca. For the Commonwealth in general, there is the Association of Commonwealth Universities' website at: http://www.acu.ac.uk/cudos.

For higher-education systems world-wide, quality assurance and accreditation issues, try: http://portal.unesco.org/education/en. For statistics on student mobility in all its forms, look up: http://www.atlas.iienetwork.org. And for world education news and reviews, there is: http://www.wes.org/ewenr/index.asp. Many of the institutions offering programmes in North America are members of BUTEX (the British Universities Transatlantic Exchange). It has a website at http://www.butex.ac.uk. Scottish students have their own guide, *International Opportunities within Scottish Education and Training*, which can be found at: http://www.scotland.gov.uk/library5/education/io03-00.asp.

The Higher Education Policy Institute website has published several helpful articles on issues concerning studying abroad, all available at http://www.hepi.ac.uk. For example, as an overview of the subject, Hatakenaka, S. (2004), 'Internationalism in Higher Education: A Review', is useful.

Of other books and articles dealing with Study Abroad, the following will provide a flavour. Many of the articles are also available electronically, if your library is a subscriber.

Altbach, Philip and Teichler, Ulrich (2001) 'Internationalization and Exchanges in a Globalized University', *Journal of Studies in International Education*, 5: 1, 5–25. This sets the subject in context and explores recent trends.

Bastick, Tony (2004) 'Commonwealth Degrees from Class to Equivalence: Changing to Grade Point Averages in the Caribbean', *Journal of Studies in International Education*, 8: 1, 86–104. Revealing on the GPA system and devastating on problems of grade translation.

Bohm, A., Davis, D., Meares, D. and Pearce, D. (2002) *Global Student Mobility 2025: Forecasts of the Global Demand for International Higher Education*, Sydney: IDP Education, Australia. The standard work of futurology in the field.

British Council (2004) *Vision 2020: Forecasting International Student Mobility: A UK Perspective*. The British view of the future.

European Journal of Education (2001) 36: 4 is devoted to 'Mobility and Co-operation in Education: Recent Experiences in Europe' and has some helpful pieces, including an interesting editorial by Ulrich Teichler and Jean Gordon on pages 397–406.

Frontiers: The Interdisciplinary Journal of Study Abroad. The house journal, entirely devoted to articles on this subject, though viewed mainly from the United States.

Hansel, Bettina (1993) *Exchange Students' Survival Kit*, Yarmouth, Maine. Intended for American high-school pupils on home-stay programmes, but is of interest to others, none the less.

McBurnie, Tony (2001) 'Globalization: A New Paradigm for Higher Education' and Kweick, Marek (2001) 'Globalization and Higher Education', *Higher Education in Europe*, 26, 11–26, 27–38. Two very different assessments of the effects of internationalism on universities.

McNamara, David and Harris, Robert (ed.) (1997) *Overseas Students in Higher Education: Issues in Teaching and Learning*, London: Routledge. An interesting, student-centred collection of articles, much concerned with educational quality.

Maiworm, Friedhelm and Teichler, Ulrich (1996) *Study Abroad and Early Career: Experiences of Former ERASMUS Students*, London: Jessica Kingsley. Mainly a work of detailed statistics, with some informed commentary.

Scott, Paul (ed.) (1998) *The Globalization of Higher Education*, Buckingham: Open University Press. An early, influential analysis of what has become a central issue.

Teather, D. C. B. (ed.) (2004) *Consortia: International Networking Alliances of Universities*, Melbourne: Melbourne University Press. The subject encompasses many Study Abroad programmes.

GLOSSARY

Educational programmes are often in a state of perpetual flux. The following terms, used in the text, may consequently be unfamiliar to some readers. Higher education today is awash with acronyms, technical verbiage and jargon, of which these form only a tiny part. None the less, this section should not be essayed by those of an irritable disposition.

academic record: an account of all the courses taken and grades obtained by students for each year of their higher education. It can be expressed in the form of a transcript.

Bologna: an EU ministerial agreement that seeks to harmonise higher-education qualifications throughout the entire organisation, using three cycles, corresponding generally to bachelor's, master's and doctoral degrees in the UK. Named after the city in which the agreement was reached. Sometimes called Prague Bologna, Berlin Bologna and Bergen Bologna, each marking further stages in the agreement, but not – yet – Bologna Bologna.

certificate of eligibility: a document used in some countries to authorise their embassies and consulates abroad to issue a student visa or residence permit. It is usually obtained by the host university and forwarded to the student.

credit: a form of educational capital which a student accrues by being adjudged to have successfully fulfilled academic requirements, such as having taken and passed a course. Normally each course has its own credit weighting. Full credit means having attended and passed all the courses required, for each stage of a programme, in order to remain in position to qualify for a specific degree award.

Diploma Supplement: an EU term for the appendage which it is proposed to attach to all bachelor and master degree parchments. This will set out, in a standardised way, the content and status of the award, ensuring that these can be understood and compared with awards elsewhere. It will include details of any study performed abroad. It is currently being rolled out across the European Union as a component of ECTS and an element in the Bologna process.

double and joint degrees: 'double' or jointly awarded degrees are those conferred simultaneously by two or more different institutions in recognition of work carried out in each as part of a single study programme, an Erasmus Mundus Master's degree, for example. Joint degrees are programmes in which students specialise in two subjects.

ECTS: European Credit Transfer System – a method employed for recording assessments of course weightings and student academic performance in EU institutions. It is meant to have relevance throughout the Union, though is not yet in use universally. It is widely employed to allow exchange students to gain credits which can substitute for degree requirements at home. The title was recently expanded to 'European Credit Transfer and Accumulation System' but the acronym remains unchanged.

Erasmus: the name given to EU programmes that enable higher-education students to study for between three months and a year in another member (or associated) state. It now forms part of the Socrates programme of educational co-operation and exchange which operates at all educational levels within the European Union. Often also known as Socrates/Erasmus or Socrates–Erasmus.

Erasmus Mundus: an EU programme for master's degree students, involving study in more than one country. Aimed at those outside and inside the member states. Operates within defined international consortia only.

exchanges: these are the procedures whereby students move, usually reciprocally, between two or more institutions in two or more different countries.

grades: academic assessments or scores or levels of attainment. Previously, 'marks' was the term most commonly used in the United Kingdom.

home status: a fee classification, indicating that the student is liable only for domestic (partial) and not for 'full' fees. The distinction relates principally to the student's place of permanent residence in the years immediately before the study commences and employs two basic categories, UK/EU and international.

IASTE: International Association for the Exchange of Students for Technical Experience. A world-wide programme, originating at Imperial College, London University, which enables science students to spend a summer period on work placements abroad.

Ivy League: a group of eight prestigious, private, east-coast institutions in the United States, widely regarded by others, as well as themselves, as forming an educational élite.

learning agreement: a statement, which has the force of a contract, issued to students departing on EU exchange programmes and setting out their agreed programme of studies while abroad. More generally used for any prior recognition of studies between student participants and partner institutions involved in an exchange.

Leonardo da Vinci: one of the many Socrates programmes of the European Union, this deals with lifelong learning (preparation for work) and vocational training (work skills). Popularly called Leonardo. Named for the Renaissance artist and inventor.

liberal arts: term used for colleges for undergraduates in the United States which offer courses in intellectual and cultural studies as opposed to professional or technical studies.

rankings: graded lists (some official, some not) of universities, which use various indicators of adjudged merit to form league tables.

semesters: divisions of the academic teaching year, generally of between thirteen and fifteen weeks in duration. There are normally two per year. In the United Kingdom, these have largely replaced 'terms', of which there were normally three per year, each of around ten weeks.

Socrates: an umbrella term for a large number of EU educational programmes, involved with educational co-operation and exchange among the member states. The term utilises the name of an ancient Greek philosopher, who became famous for his eccentric teaching method.

TEMPUS: another of the EU educational co-operation programmes, this is now directed mainly at the successor states of the former Soviet Union, the Balkans and eastern and southern Mediterranean countries. It is aimed at helping the process of social and economic reform and the development of higher education there.

transcript: an official university document, recording a student's academic performance. It generally includes lists of courses taken and grades obtained.

work placement: a form of employment, typically undertaken abroad, giving students vocational experience and cultural immersion.

INDEX